God and Plastic Surgery

Marx, Nietzsche, Freud and the Obvious

A Book

GOD AND PLASTIC SURGERY

MARX, NIETZSCHE, FREUD AND THE OBVIOUS

A BOOK

JEREMY BARRIS

Contents

Preface 7
General Introduction 19

Part One
Introduction to the Eulogy 25
Eulogy: How to Speak Well
    For Socrates 31
Prologue and Poem 109

Part Two
Introduction to Part Two 111
In Freud's Defense:ɘƨuɘʇɘᗡ ƨ'buɘɿᖷ uI
    In Freud's Defense..................................... 117
Afterthought to Part Two 175

Part Three
Introduction to Impotence 179
The Impotence of Being Earnest 185
To Keats 211

Notes 213

Dedication

To my parents, for being such bad parents, and in honour of whose integrity I
was such a bad son, or perhaps such a good daughter

To Stephanie and Wittgenstein, for giving me pause for thought, and
to Nadine and Sukie, for giving me thought to pause, and
to Steve, for being there in the middle

To Christian, for not writing

To Jeff, for teaching me Jim, and for correcting me.

And, of course, to Roy Blumenthal.

Preface

I give an account in this book of living justly. The motive for doing this is to establish the possibility of living in such a way that one can honestly feel a sense of dignity and honestly feel that one is making a worthwhile contribution to others and to the society in which one's life participates.

I am not assuming an unlikely or rare altruism. One is not simply a part of society; but one's self, *especially* at its most unrelated to society as a whole, *is* in part made up of one's relations both to others and to society in general.

To get the sense of this one has to abandon thinking of self and society in the way one thinks of material objects.

Self and society are the kind of thing which can be entirely unrelated to each other *and* entirely parts of each other, at one and the same time.

One can't think of objects that way, because these are incompatible statements to make about objects. But self and society can *only* be thought of that way, and to think of these statements as incompatible in connection with self and society very soon shows itself not to make sense.

At least, that's the way I understand it. The choice appears to me to be between thinking about self and society this way, or to make a commitment to making mistakes continually and never to learn from them.

I am not, then, assuming altruism. I am assuming that altruism and being self-serving go together, so that one can be proud of oneself only if one can be proud of one's behaviour and attitudes towards others and towards society at large.

This does not mean that one is unselfish by being self-

7

ish. It does mean that very frequently what we think of, in our technological and object-oriented age, as selfishness is in fact altruism, and the other way around. Before we can establish what selfishness and unselfishness are, then, we first have to think about self and others in the way suited to them, and then come back and think properly about the labels with which we started.

As I said, I give an account here of living justly, to establish the possibility of living with honest pride. But not to be proud of living justly. That should be taken for granted as a bare minimum of responsible or respectworthy life. One should be ashamed if one does *not* live justly. I concentrate here on the possibility of living justly because that is the precondition, and *only* the precondition, of being proud of oneself in whatever one's exceptional accomplishments happen to be.

Living justly is what allows one *honestly* to feel dignity, worth and pride. It's one's way of not imposing oneself unfairly on others and on oneself (and these two, as I've said, go together). That is, it's one's way of letting things be what they are in human affairs. That is why it's the precondition for honesty: one can only be honest if it is possible to leave and see things as they are. Living justly *means* letting things be what they are.

The practice of justice is therefore the equivalent in everyday life of scientific method or epistemology. One can do someone, oneself, or a society or culture justice or injustice, and one can do the facts or a theory or a point of view justice or injustice. In the end, living justly has bearing also on the way of understanding material objects. Good ecology considers this in very specific detail.

Living justly, then, is the precondition of living honestly and of thinking correctly. It is the precondition, that is, of being true to oneself and also of true thought. It is the requirement of both everyday life and philosophy.

People may object that generosity of sympathy, and

not justice, is the really important thing. I agree.

But one must know the difference between what is right and what is more than enough. If one does not, then one is not only going to be unaware of when one does both oneself *and* others injustice, under the mistaken impression of being better than just, but one is also *going to do* such injustice.

If one wants to encourage the possibility of others honestly being proud of themselves, one must obviously avoid doing this in a way which humiliates them from the start. If one is generous to people who lack the understanding to be generous, to be reasonably expected to be generous, in return, one is patronising them and insulting them. One is letting them know, in the strongest possible way — by one's own actions — that, as far as oneself is concerned, their entire way of living and doing things is not good enough.

Gandhi's peaceful resistance, for example, was not an act of love towards humankind as represented by the British. It was an act of extreme moral violence. As I understand it. It was a striking display of disrespect for an entire culture, and its demoralising effects were demonstrated by the result.

This is not to say that Gandhi was not justified. On the contrary, he acted perfectly justly. But he did not act more than justly, with a generous enlargement of sympathy.

To do that he would have had to act with what would normally have been mere justice, and no more than that, so as not to attack and do violence to the very principle of the culture he opposed.

When one is dealing, that is, with a way of life which is genuinely based, for example, on different values from one's own, the way to be more than just, to be loving, or to be constructive and encourage future reconciliation or the best for both parties independently in the future, is simply to be what is otherwise only just. One has to do only what is right, and no more than enough.

If one understands this, but refuses to do it, then it is

perhaps because one is not content with the ordinary, the unimpressive, and wants to be spectacular, and to look good. And if that is the case, then one is truly being selfish, and putting one's own trivial gain over both the other's and one's own vital concerns.

One can't be held responsible for one's actions before one has had a genuine opportunity to know what one is doing. But once one has had that opportunity, one *is* then responsible, whether one is held so or not. One can then return and think properly about the labels with which one started.

What is very important to realise, as I understand it, is that what appears to be love can in fact serve hatred, although one only finds that out once an opportunity to know what one is doing arises. The reverse is also true.

This allows me to say that this book, while it is a baroque book on justice, is a minimalist book on love. Bearing in mind that hatred, bitterness and anger can be ways of loving, this book, through all its clamorous verbosity and stylistic ostentation, maintains throughout a tasteful silence on what is in fact its chief topic, saying only what is absolutely necessary to convey its point with precision.

And it is perhaps the faults and excesses of the book which enable the treatment of its topic without the ruination of that topic merely by the fact of its being treated with rigour.

This is not an apology for the faults and excesses to be found here. I am not sure, in any event, that for a philosopher they need apology. I'm not sure that they are faults. I'm not sure, either, that it is not better if they are faults.

This book, then, deals with living justly, in the very peculiar circumstances of being faced with a way of life very different from one's own. It does so because this peculiar circumstance is becoming a norm in our culture(s). This does not stand in the way of similarity of oulook remaining a norm which also needs to be understood. But justice under the conditions of that normal norm is already very much discussed and thought through. I therefore focus on justice in the other circumstances of very different ways of life.

Both these norms can co-exist in one person's life, and do, given that people participate in the life of their society, and our society has both these norms. This, as I understand it, is the ethical significance of psychoanalysis and psychotherapy. One learns to relate to oneself as to someone whom one has to learn to understand.

I have devoted the second section to discussing Freud, for this reason, with a view to showing how the logic of psychoanalysis, properly thought through, is the logic, in the individual focus, of what, in the social focus, is justice — and hence honesty, and hence the possibility of genuine pride.

The biggest challenge to the ideas of pride, honesty, and dignity comes from the anti-humanist strain of much contemporary thought, which insists that human individuals are not the centre of the way things work, and do not significantly decide either their own destinies or that of their society. Something else does: technology, material conditions, language, differentials of force or power, varieties of the unconscious.

I think this is entirely true. I also think that it is entirely false. I have consequently attempted to describe the workings of justice, understood as the basis for honesty, dignity and pride, in the terms of anti-humanism taken as correct, as a true description of the way the world is.

Again, it is a matter of understanding human concerns in the way suited to those concerns. If drives, for example, are to explain human concerns, they must be capable of providing an explanation of those concerns, and that means that we must understand drives as being as interesting and subtle as the interests and subtleties they explain. Otherwise they simply do not explain human concerns, and there is no reason to regard them as in any way basic to those concerns.

First we must understand what we're trying to explain, and then — and *only* then — we can come back and think properly about the labels with which we started. If caring for others, for example, is purely a roundabout way of gratifying our entirely selfish desire to feel good about ourselves or to have power, then *caring for others* is what gratifies our selfish desire and makes us feel powerful. Our "selfish" desire *is* then what we *mean* by an *unselfish* desire, and power *means* what we mean by genuine care.

Again, it is a matter of understanding human affairs by recognising that what is incompatible in the case of objects is mistakenly separated in the case of human affairs. One has to think the otherwise incompatible things together from the start, and then return to think properly about the separate ideas, the ones belonging to the explanation and those belonging to what is explained.

And again, this is important when very different kinds of idea are put together, just as the incompatibilities seen in the idea of justice are important when very different ways of life are faced with one another.

Some schools of thought refuse to put different kinds of ideas together. Other schoools of thought put them together without thinking about it too hard. I suggest that one needs to put them together while recognising from the start that they don't go together. That way they shed light on each other, keep each other interesting and capable of growth, change and fresh possibilities, while not distorting and falsifying each other.

This procedure has traditionally been the province of art. In the last section I try to show why aesthetic sensibility, in its own terms taken as true description of the way the world is, is significant for living justly, in its own way, in the way suited to it.

I have chosen the Romantic conception of aesthetic sensibility for this. I could have started with any other, and then I would have said something very different.

But this is a philosophical book, not a guide to right conduct, a manual for conducting psychoanalyses, or a prescription for what is aesthetically right.

My concern is to discuss the way in which what we already do in these affairs makes sense in connection with justice, to the best of my ability. When I say "we must...", that is because I am describing an ethical issue, or an issue which already has a prescription in it. If one is not interested in taking responsibility for oneself, then this book is simply not worth reading. If one is, then I am describing, not prescribing, throughout.

I could have discussed knowledge, or Freud, or aesthetic sensibility in any number of different ways, and consequently would have said very different things to what I say here.

But for the purposes which this thinking serves, these possibilities make no difference. They would each have provided detailed examples with which to show and discuss the details of how living and thinking justly make sense, can be understood, where very different ways of life or very different kinds of idea find themselves together.

The advantage of concentrating, in the final section, on the Romantic conception of aesthetic sensibility is that this is the humanistic perspective *par excellence*, and allows the logic already displayed in moving from anti-humanistic concerns to humanistic concerns, to be displayed in moving from humanistic concerns to humanistic concerns which go immediately with anti-humanistic concerns. That, at least, was the intention.

Given all of this, let me say that, in my opinion, the introductions to the various parts of the book are the most philosophically interesting thing to be found here. They are not concerned to elaborate the details of a thought, but simply to specify the thought and leave it with its evocativeness. The rest of the book is intended, also, to be as evocative as possible without destroying the continuity of the line of thought.

But the rest of the book, because of the lengthy continuity, hides the entirely alternative ways of framing and pursuing the whole topic, the ways, also, of subordinating it to the discussion of topics which are subordinated in discussing this one.

Most important, it hides the simple *fact that* there *are* alternative ways, and with that fact, it hides the enormous significance of the awareness of that simple fact.

This book is concerned to explore the significance of that "fact that" there is more than one way of understanding things, when it *is* a fact. The details of the points of view chosen, and which viewpoints are chosen, to discuss their joint existence are less important, for the present purposes, than the mere fact that they do exist jointly, when they do.

This book not only tries to make sense of living justly; it also tries to do justice to making sense, on the basis of the sense of justice.

Together with the value of the continuous discussion made possible by a single book, then, this book has the defect of containing only the continuous discussion made possible by a single book. For that reason, it is automatically wrong, simply by the bare fact of its having the length and self-containment it does.

If that is borne in mind, it is not, I think, wrong any longer. That is why, in my opinion, the introductions are the most philosophically interesting parts of it. If they leave one with the impression that they are true, they also do so with an immediate and easy evocation of what else might be said.

This book will not be true, then, until the reader has an immediate and easy idea of what else, very different, might be said.

In our talk about politics, society or conduct, or about science itself, in all branches of philosophy including psychology, in all discussions of art, literature, language, truth, beauty and the good, our principal terms incessantly change their meanings with the sentences they go into and the contexts they derive from. We are all ready enough to suspect this, if not in our own talk at least in that of our fellows, and ready to see in it a chief cause for the lamented fact that these subjects show — once we have allowed for current fashions — strangely little progress. But both the extent *and the plan* of these deluding shifts are hidden from us by the assumption I am attacking. It leads us to think that a shift of meaning is a flaw in discourse , a regrettable accident, instead of a virtue. And therefore we neglect to study the plan of these shifts.

The assumption is that words have, or should have, proper meanings which people should recognize, agree about and stick to. A pretty program, if it were possible. But, outside the technical languages of the sciences, it is not possible. For in the topics with which all generally interesting discussion is concerned, words must shift their meanings thus. Without these shifts such mutual understanding as we achieve would fail even within the narrowed resultant scope. Language, losing its subtlety with its suppleness, would lose also its power to serve us.

The remedy is not to resist these shifts but to learn to follow them. They recur in the same forms with different words; they have similar places and common patterns , which experience enables us to observe and obey in practice...

I. A. Richards,
The Philosophy of Rhetoric.[1]

The work of the philosopher consists in assembling reminders for a particular purpose.

Wittgenstein
Philosophical Investigations, §127

...we are not contributing curiosities..., but observations which no one has doubted, but which have escaped remark only because they are always before our eyes.

Wittgenstein
Philosophical Investigations, §415

God and Plastic Surgery
Marx, Nietzsche, Freud and the Obvious

A Book

General Introduction to the Book

The argument and structure of this book may be taken to be an elaboration of the relevance to contemporary political, ethical and aesthetic thought of the following consideration. If one is struggling to decide whether, in a given situation, something is truly the case or its opposite — or something else — is truly the case, then one can be quite sure that the general area to which these somethings belong is in some way important to one, is in some way an issue for one.

One knows it is important to one, simply because finds oneself struggling; and one knows it is that general area which is in some way important to one, because, whichever of the alternatives may in fact be the case, one finds oneself struggling in the area presupposed or defined by both of them.

This is different from wondering, for example, *how* something could be the case, or *when* something would be or was the case, or *why* something is the case. These examples all certainly involve a *decision* that the *something* is definitely the case, but the previous example certainly involves a decision that the *general area* to which the somethings belong is in some way important to one, that questions and answers about that *kind* of something are important to one.

In other words , if it is important to one that one can't find an answer to one's questions or question, one at least knows with certainty that the area with which the questions are concerned is important to one. The fact of insistently asking the question then itself becomes a source of a different kind of answer, to a different kind of question, reached in a different kind of way.

Some of the differences are as follows. The enquiry is directed towards oneself, rather than outwards; it goes backwards, as it were. The answers present themselves immediately in what one finds oneself doing in attempting to answer the questions, or *in the fact that* one finds oneself attempting to answer those particular questions; and finding the right questions becomes the difficult thing to do. And the whole process keeps reversing itself, or shifting tangentially from general area of concern to general area of concern, or shifting levels to and from general areas from and to specific alternatives presupposing general areas, or shifting levels *and* rotating from and to an opposition of alternatives to and from an opposition of general areas; and so on.

This reversing and shifting of the process means that this kind of enquiry includes the kind of enquiry — simply going about finding answers to questions — from which I differentiated it.

On the way, one is likely to find answers to the original question with which one was struggling. But the point of this consideration is that when one kind of familiar way of questioning brings one to a point of undecidability, a different kind of questioning is made possible precisely *by* that undecidability, without which one's motivation to struggle with that particular kind of issue would not have an opportunity to demonstrate itself.

And the point is also — includes — that the undecidability can be resolved by abandoning the line of enquiry which led to it and adopting a kind of line of enquiry irrelevant to the original issue, although significant in its own way and for its own kind of purposes. There is, therefore, a kind of connection between the two kinds of enquiry, a way or a sense or a kind of case or situation in which the irrelevant can be relevant, and the relevant irrelevant, in which the tangential can be as directly to the point as possible, and vice-versa, in which a shift and a rotation can be equivalent to a straight line, and vice-versa, and in which the frivolous, abrupt and clumsy can be as serious, smooth and skilful as we could want or need, and vice-versa.

A fascination with the working or logic of this alternative way of enquiry, and with how to articulate that working or logic, how to articulate the precision of and the relation between the ways in which it shifts; with the relation between this alternative way of enquiry and the familiar ways of enquiry; and with the ways in which it supports and limits the familiar kind of enquiry: this fascination is the motive for the present book. That, and, perhaps as importantly, a fascination and a less self-involved concern with the relevance of these three areas of consideration, taken together, for contemporary political, ethical and aesthetic thought.

These two fascinations are not really separate: it is in the attempt to deal with the problems of ethical, aesthetic, and political life that these two fascinations and concerns arise as alternatives; they presuppose or define that general area — and in a very tricky sense of unity, I do think it is *a* general area — as that to which they belong. An insistent struggle to answer a question, after all , indicates that the question is important to one, and an insistence that is genuinely important to one — a commitment — to finding a truth, is an ethical commitment, perhaps *the* ethical commitment *par excellence*, and perhaps the basis of ethical commitment in general.

From which, as Aristotle said, follows politics, and from that, thinking about thinking in general. And which comes first? It depends, perhaps, on who one is, and what one is doing, and where and when and why and with whom one is doing it, and to what degree any of these considerations is important at the time. And so on. In the end, perhaps, it's a matter of taste.

In any event, one can but try. If one succeeds, one's success will be only for that place, for that time, for the person one is and for the people among whom one is at that time and in that place.

So that, in any event, one can but try. If one fails, one's failure will only be…

It is the fully acknowledged particularity and contextualisation of a thought or work which allows whatever universality it might have: since all particular contexts have universally in common the *fact that* they are particular contexts. It is by not attempting universality that one might succeed in achieving it.

As I said, in any event, one can but try.

And where, it may be asked, other than in thinking, is the practical or applied side of this? A friend of mine once made clear to me that there is a difference between being selfish and being able to admit that one is selfish. And I worked out for myself that there is a difference between different manners in which one is able to admit it. If one is unable to admit it , one is unlikely to want to acknowledge even that there is a difference between being selfish and being able to admit that one is selfish. The capacity for the theory presupposes the attempt to engage in the practice.

Part One

Eulogy: How to Speak Well

For Socrates

Introduction to Part One

In the words of George Bernard Shaw:

It may seem a long way from Bunyan to Nietzsche; but the difference between their conclusions is merely formal. Bunyan's perception that righteousness is filthy rags, his scorn for Mr Legality in the village of Morality, his defiance of the Church as the supplanter of religion, his insistence on courage as the virtue of virtues, his estimate of the career of the conventionally respectable and sensible Worldly Wiseman as no better at bottom that the life and death of Mr Badman: all this, expressed by Bunyan in the terms of a tinker's theology, is what Nietzsche has expressed in terms of post-Darwin, post-Schopenhauer philosophy; Wagner in terms of polytheistic mythology; and Ibsen in terms of mid-XIX century Parisian dramaturgy. Nothing is new in these matters except their novelties: for instance, it is a novelty to call Justification by Faith "Wille," and Justification by Works "Vorstellung." The sole use of the novelty is that you and I buy and read Schopenhauer's treatise on Will and Representation when we should not dream of buying a set of sermons on Faith versus Works. At bottom the controversy is the same, and the dramatic results are the same.[1]

Truth is a very strange thing. It is, of course, always the truth as the presenter of that truth sees it. And it is that as the presenter sees it at the time, with the intellectual, rhetorical and stylistic devices with which to articulate it which the presenter has at his/her disposal at that time, and with the capacity which s/he has at the time to identify and articulate with precision what the truth is that s/he wants to say or present. But the truth for a particular person is not *just* the truth for a particular person. The truth for a particular person is the most profoundly important kind of truth for us, in a sense the *only* kind of truth which has meaning for us, with which we can do anything, since we are all, as it happens, particular people.

This is not to say that there are no general truths. It is to say, rather, that general truths are still general truths *for particular people*. If we regard something as generally true, we can only responsibly do so if we ourselves, or particular people whom we ourselves have reason to regard as reliable or trustworthy, have personally investigated the relevant matters in a responsible and valid way, so as to discover and ensure the general truth of this something. Even in the case of religious truths, one can only be an advocate of a general religious truth if one is prepared to bear witness to its validity personally, either in the responsible attempt to understand one's own experience and to relate it to the experience of others; or in one's actions; or in the simple fact of one's having attempted to make a certain commitment in a responsibly sustained manner.

And if a general truth has meaning for us, then that already says that it is a general truth specifically *for us*. The constraints which govern what we are capable of meaning, understanding and finding meaningful also constrain what we mean when we present that general truth or articulate it or understand it for ourselves. It can only mean for us what we are capable of meaning or finding meaningful or understandable. If a general truth has any meaning for us, then, it is *only* a general truth *for us*. And if it has no meaning for us, then there is no point in regarding it as a general truth: we can't make any real sense of it, let alone do anything with it.

But a general truth is not *just* the general truth for us. A general truth for us is the *only kind* of general truth, in a sense, which has meaning for us. It therefore fulfills everything which general truths have ever fulfilled, which have had meaning for us.

The presentation of a truth, like truth itself, is a very strange thing. When we are different, at different points of our lives, in different circumstances, concerned with different people, in different moods, in different social and cultural environments, the same truth can only be accurately presented in different ways. Rhetoric, style, and the composition of what one is presenting are therefore an essential part of the presentation of truth. They are therefore also an essential part of the working of truth itself, since truth is only truth in practice by being presented, even if only presented to ourselves. Truth is only really truth as some particular person or people see(s) it, whether it is discovered or whether it is brought about.

If it is there before we see it, before we have it presented, there is no point talking about it, since we haven't yet seen it: it does not yet have a meaning for us. Whether it is discovered or whether it is brought about, then, truth is meaningful only when we can talk about it or show it; and it needs to be presented in different ways at different times particularly if it is to remain the same: and the way in which we talk about it is therefore an essential part of the working of truth.

There are times and circumstances in which the presentation of a truth, the rhetoric, style and composition, are *all* that is essential to the working of the truth being presented. When a certain kind of presentation of the truth in question has been long familiar, and the circumstances change sufficiently, a new presentation or kind of presentation becomes necessary. At a point in this development, it can be that the old presentation itself becomes the primary obstacle to the accurate or meaningful presentation of the same kind of truth, as it must be presented to be meaningful to us in the changed circumstances. At that point the truth about presentation itself is what needs primarily to be presented, as that truth is itself accurately or meaningfully to be presented at the time and for us at the time.

The same thing is the case under circumstances in which the familiar forms of presentation are unsuited to present a perception which is in some sense new. And the same thing is the case when it is important, for whatever reasons, to present only the *fact of* communication, bare of any particular content other than itself. The most difficult art in the field of rhetoric is that of communicating nothing. This is so despite the frequency with which writers and speakers are in fact found to excel in this most difficult accomplishment. As Oscar Wilde put it, "Only the great masters of style ever succeed in being obscure."[2]

When there is a great deal at stake, either for the presenter of the truth or for those to whom it is presented or both; and when the familiar mode of presentation is not only unsuited to the presentation of the truth, but is designed specifically to hinder or prevent that presentation; and when sufficient change of circumstances on either or both sides has been undergone, to make the presentation of a new mode of presentation possible: the presentation of the bare fact of presentation or communication itself can be the best thing to do. A simple "oh" can, under circumstances like this, be the most telling, penetrating and thoroughgoing piece of rhetorical workpersonship, either by way of affirmation, or of devastation, or of ingenious non-committal. And silence can be a rather humourless, unimaginative and insipid way of doing the same thing — which may, of course, be what is required.

The choice of the right or most suitable images, ideas, words, attitudes, statements and kinds of argument for that tricky point of presentation of presentation depends on the mode of presentation which precedes or is on one side of that point as being familiar, and on the mode of presentation which follows or is on the other side of that point as being a necessary new way of saying the same thing, or as an old way appropriate to saying a new thing, or as a way of saying a different thing, or as all three of these.

And the familiar way of presenting which precedes or is on one side of that point, and the new or becoming-familiar way of presenting which follows or is on the other side of that point, depend in their turn for their suitability on the truths, respectively, which precede and follow that point, or which are, respectively, on one side or the other of that point. The choice of the right or most suitable images, ideas, words, attitudes, statements, kinds of argument and the mutual disposition of all of these, for the point at which rhetoric, style and composition are all that is, for the time, essential to the working of the truth that is being presented, therefore depends fully on the truth or truths in question, as it or they are when their particular form of presentation does not matter so much.

But if one is to understand that dependence, and get the point, both of the unfamiliar presentation and of the familiar one in its relation to the unfamiliar one, one must be prepared to be or to become able fully to appreciate the way in which rhetoric, style, and compostition work, and how they work in relation to the presentation of truth, and in just what kinds of ways truth requires rhetoric, style, and composition for its truthful working and presentation. One must be or become able, that is, to suspend one's judgment and one's certainties about how what can be said. And the first reward is an opportunity to appreciate an art, whether it is an art of doing a certain kind of work or a work of a certain kind of art.

In any event, as George Bernard Shaw said, "After all, the main thing in determining the artistic quality of a book is not the opinions it propagates, but the fact that the writer has opinions."[3] And with that, I submit for your serious consideration the following attempt to come to terms with contemporary political, ethical and socially critical thought, as it is largely to be found in the works of such people as Althusser, Foucault, Baudrillard, Derrida, Lacan, Winch, MacIntyre, Gadamer, and Hocquenghem. The most entertaining essay on contemporary matters of this kind that I have so far found, as well as being solidly and spontaneously thought-provoking without requiring an immense labour to find out what it's supposed to mean, is John Cuddihy's *The Ordeal of Civility: Freud, Marx, Lévi-Strauss, and the Jewish Struggle with Modernity*.[4]

Eulogy: How to Speak Well

for Socrates

Knowledge is a form of power. We are told this by Marx, Nietzsche, and Freud.

Marx tells us this by explaining that the working class can only achieve its revolutionary potential by becoming for itself what it already is in itself, that is, by becoming conscious of itself as an exploited class of people, and not merely remaining a collection of individuals isolated in their unexplained and endured suffering. Only when each individual in the working class rebels against his or her suffering because it is understood as a symptom of exploitation, and therefore as unjust or unreasonable and as requiring abolition, and because it is understood as a symptom common to the majority of the population, who therefore *can* abolish it provided they act together as a unified force, only then is the class fully a class, for itself and in itself. It is the understanding, the conscious knowledge, which allows both the change of attitude from one of endurance to one of revolt, and the uniting of individuals into a class with common interests and mutual support. Knowledge is therefore an essential component of the taking up of power. The act of knowing is

31

the act of taking up a position of opposition or criticism: this becomes a position of power when enough people know. Until enough people know, although they really are a class of people, that reality is not complete, it doesn't have the power or effectiveness of full reality, simply because knowledge is absent.

Marx tells us that this knowledge or consciousness cannot arrive until the material conditions have prepared the way for it, that is, until it is really possible to remove the exploitation, so that the knowledge has some practical value. Dialectically, the material conditions cannot change until the conscious interests of people change it. And so there's a back and forth movement between the way things are and what is known about the way things are, a back and forth movement leading to a coincidence of knowledge and reality, at which point reality becomes complete and power enters the hands of those to whom it belongs, being the majority.

Nietzsche tells us that knowledge is a form of power by explaining that everything is a form of power; the workings of power are the center of his concern. He circumscribes it within a circle described by the eternal return of the same, which knowledge can only appreciate and repeat. A movement of departure and return, a forth and back movement which goes nowhere except into the experience of a few, otherwise meaningless and, in the case of the few, ugly, beautiful and absurd, superfluous, unnecessary in its experienced necessity.

Freud tells us that knowledge is a form of power by explaining that what one does not know about oneself is what destroys one most effectively, and that the only way to have one's strength at one's disposal is to acquire the relevant knowledge of oneself. And one can only get to know by allowing oneself not to know for long enough to get to know something different from what one already, mistakenly, knows, and then to catch oneself and interpret oneself in a new way, and then to keep on not knowing, and interpret in a new way, until there's a coincidence between what one is and what one knows oneself to be. At that point the reality of what one is is less weakened by opposition between what it is and what it knows, and power falls into the hands of effective activity. The act of knowing is the act of becoming effective (or powerful) in the path of one's desire, and it can only turn out that way via a back-and-forth movement between knowledge and reality, since one can't know until one can bear the knowledge and one can only progress towards bearing the knowledge by changing oneself at each point with a fraction of that knowledge.

All three of these thinkers opposed their knowledge to an existing form of knowledge. What each of them was saying divided itself into two parts: what they were saying which was their own independent concern, the way they thought a particular aspect of the world works, and what they were saying about the knowledge which opposed them. And both of these parts had to do with knowledge about knowledge. The first part attempted to know something new about knowledge (it's a piece of the system of economic domination or economic reasonableness, it's a dishonest mask of the will to power or an honest mask of the will to power, it's an effective form of sexuality and aggression or it's an ineffective form of sexuality and aggression). The second part attempted to know this new thing about knowledge from the point of view of the knowledge which opposed it, that is, to prove itself to be knowledge in a way convincing to the opposition, in the opposition's terms. Marx did it by critique, Nietzsche did it by innuendo, Freud did it by using the language and method of science.

But they all sought knowledge, and they all sought to overcome a certain knowledge, and they all sought both of these things by means of knowledge, whether it was theirs or that of the opposition. And what was crucial to settle, for all of them, was what is involved in understanding understanding, having conscious knowledge of conscious knowledge, being self-conscious. What would knowledge look like which was knowledge of that point at which knowledge and reality coincided?

Knowledge is a form of power. It adds something to what was there before the knowledge, and by that simple fact it changes things, makes what is there different at least by the addition of knowledge to what is there. There are two situations in which this statement is not true as it stands. The first is the situation in which the knowledge is universally known and accepted as the only knowledge, or accepted as knowledge (rather than belief or supposition) by the holders of power or by a large enough proportion of the population or a sufficiently influential part of the population for the knowledge to be taken as the only knowledge pertinent to the workings of the world. Then the knowledge adds nothing. It is already there, and is already part of what is there, and no greater degree of certainty can be arrived at. And then it is most powerful, because it excludes completely and beyond the possibility of question what it does not know, since there is no other knowledge: it knows everything there is to be known. It is powerless as seen from within, but it is crushingly powerful as seen from without, since whatever happens which is not included in the knowledge is not recognised or registered as something to be known: such things do not enter consciousness. If excluded things do find a way of entering consciousness, they enter under the aspect of shock or that which is to be shunned, abhorred, avoided: ghosts, witches, insanity, dreams which are not remembered.

The second situation is that in which the conditions of life, the material conditions, do not allow for any but a few to have any direct or indirect use for the knowledge. Then the knowledge adds a great deal, since it runs counter to all the knowledge which is already a part of what is there. It is very powerful from within, but powerless from without, since it is not recognised or registered as dealing with something to be known, given that it cannot play any part in the lives of any but the few.

These are both extreme positions. They imply that knowledge can effectively legislate what is taken as reality, making it an academic and pointless question whether reality really works that way. If everyone, or nearly everyone, *knows* that the world is like that, then, as far as human reality is concerned, the world is like that, and assertions to the contrary are pointless aberration. Demonstrations to the contrary merely indicate a distortion of reality in the perceiver or the perceived.

Knowledge is a form of power. It does not merely allow us to predict and control. It *is* a form of control. It controls what is allowed to be real without shock or tremendous conflict within the personality. If we live in a society in which everything is known to work in the way that three dimensional objects work, then everything effectively works that way. I am what I am, I can't change my feelings. My emotions are there, like an object, and may decompose in time, like an object. This is the kind of person I am and I can't change. This is different from saying, for example, I'm a heterosexual and I don't want to be homosexual, or I've tried but couldn't, or why should I? I want a cigarette. Are you sure it isn't someone else in the room who wants a cigarette? Answer the telephone. Perhaps it's you calling to tell yourself something through someone else's mouth. Why not? It happens in dreams.

The most powerful way for knowledge to work, seen from the outside, is to be taken for granted as obvious. Who would bother to question the obvious? And on what basis would you question the obvious? After all, if you're going to prove something, you have to *base* your proof on the obvious, either what can be seen by everyone or what everyone already accepts as obviously true. All people have sex drives. I don't. Well, you're not a person, everyone knows that. I am and I don't. Prove it. Prove that I do. You have an erection. That's only because my eye's sore.

And the most powerful way for knowledge to work, seen from the inside, is for it to be extremely surprising. It's easy to find the practical implications of something surprising, where the practical implications, suggesting different ways of doing things and different attitudes towards old things, are very hard to find in the case of obvious knowledge, since what makes the knowledge obvious is that its implications for everyday life have become taken for granted themselves.

When knowledge is taken for granted as obvious, it can *only* be seen to work as power from the outside. Precisely because it's taken for granted, it can't be seen to work from the inside, it can only be seen as knowledge, like an object which is just there, which doesn't work in any particular way, except how it's made to work by its possessors. That's why it's most powerful — it's excluded even knowledge of its own working, so that the current knowledge about knowledge will not say that it works *as* power, only that it gives you access to *other* things which are powerful. Same as time is money.

When knowledge is very surprising, it can only be seen to work as power from the inside. From the outside, it doesn't look like knowledge, but like aberration, dysfunction, wild speculation, or frivolity.

So in the case of obvious knowledge the problem is to be convinced that it's power. And in the case of surprising knowledge, the problem is to be convinced that it's knowledge. In other words, the problem in the first case is not knowledge — that's sorted out to everyone's satisfaction. The problem is power, and what to do with it. And the problem in the second case is not power — you just follow your own personal ethics, since your power is your own and not that of the community at large. The problem is knowledge, and what to do with it. And in each case the very thing which is the problem is partly hidden in the thing which is clearly not the problem, and in each case the very thing which is the problem is recognised for what it is only in the context of the other case, in which it is clearly not the problem.

Which is why Marx, Nietzsche, and Freud all had to settle the problem of self-consciousness, knowledge about knowledge, because the most unsettling thing not to have settled is what was until recently taken most for granted. Particularly when what was taken most for granted happened to be the basis of your power over reality, and happened to be the basis of your power over reality only *because* you took it for granted, and you discover this fully and surely for the first time only now that you don't take it for granted any more, which you don't, since you can only see what you took for granted from the outside, so that suddenly the basis of your power over reality isn't there any more, before you were in a position to know it, and precisely *because* you succeeded in your aim of knowing it, and before you have anything other than knowledge to work with. So this all comes as something of an emotional surprise, and the problem of knowing what to do with knowledge becomes important. A class' knowledge of its own radically public consciousness, a person's knowledge about his or her own radically important knowledge, a person's knowledge about her or his own radically private knowledge.

All, of course, at the extremes, because that is where the taken for granted stops, and the obvious can be put in question. The meeting place between the two extremes is where the most obvious becomes the most surprising, which is a bummer for those who wanted an easy ride.

Private and public, personal and social, important and unimportant: priorities are thrown in question at the same time as knowledge itself, the old names no longer apply in the same places, the way to re-apply them has lost its power of certainty, and until the names are put back or into right places there's no way to know which actions and which thoughts are in the name of the priorities and values one has so far worked toward.

Knowledge is a form of power. It is well known that the twentieth century, the age of late capitalism, global communication, universally accessible information, is a century lacking in the unknowable. There is nothing that has not been, or cannot be, explained. Rightly or wrongly, an explanation can in principle and in fact be found for the functioning of other cultures, our own society, language, emotions, instincts, thinking, the body, matter and energy, the universe, the global eco-system, the media, dreams, ghosts, witches, insanity, criminality, aberration, normality, customs, art, myth, rituals, fashion, power, domination, rebellion, sickness, war, peace, health, history and knowledge. And each of these can be explained in terms of any of the others, and frequently has been.

By means of explanation the twentieth century has taken control of every cultural and human phenomenon that has been available over the globe and in history, including some that haven't happened yet. In this way, by not taking these phenomena for granted, we have brought ourselves to see them only from the outside, and we have thereby removed the power over reality which they possessed. Since we are doing the same to our own culture, we are removing the power over reality which our own knowledge possesses and, increasingly, we are losing any sense of reality at all. We do not see this, because we are on the inside, and take our knowledge for granted as the only knowledge of reality which is to be taken seriously. But what we know as reality is not what was known as reality fifty years ago. It is becoming extremely hard to distinguish between human beings and computers or word-processors, except that computers are on the whole more efficient, more complex, less mindlessly brutal, and more dramatic. Who stars in the movies? The human race is disappearing as of any significance to the working of this world.

I think that this is an excellent thing. It is tragic, unbelievably horrifying, and universally murderous. But it is not remarkably different from the rest of human history in that respect. All religion testifies to that, as does all art, all philosophy and all everyday existence. They all embody a longing for a better world, and elaborate means of escaping from this one.

There is a tendency among the *avant-garde*, following in the footsteps of Nietzsche, to deprecate the world history of mysticism, metaphysics and rationality as a mystifying nihilism which attempts to deny this world in favour of one that doesn't exist. The exemplary illustration of this is Nietzsche's criticism of Socrates for having a cock sacrificed, on his death, to Asclepius, godling of medicine. This, says Nietzsche, is a calumniation of life, accusing it of being a disease. But this is a crass error on Nietzsche's part. Life *is* a disease, the universe would be considerably less difficult without it, and what Nietzsche never considered, in his quest for health, was whether disease was perhaps not a good thing, not as a road to recovery, or in the sense in which pregnancy is an illness, but as disease. Nietzsche would have benefited by being more Aristotelian. It was Nietzsche who was denying life, in favour of something that it isn't, and not Socrates.

Socrates, like mysticism, metaphysics and rationality, accepted what life was *and* tried to do something about it, in the same act. It's horrible, let's escape. Nietzsche wanted truth and honesty, which is abhorrently vulgar. I'm a poet and I lie, he said. Okay, nauseate me. Get your revenge on me, because you can't stand truth enough to ignore it and hide it well. Grow up, Nietzsche, and learn to enjoy being a kid. Socrates could.

Perhaps disease is a good thing. De Sade thought so, Masoch thought so, and Pauline Réage thought so. And there's nothing to be said to any of them; they're all irrefutable. They're very powerful. They know where to put knowl-

edge, as any decent pervert would. The anus is a very ne-
glected opening, and for very good reason: its function puts
reality before shame and dignity, and if you deny it successfully you become poisoned and poisonous. The anus is a
very humiliating organ. Which is why it's the most dreadful
and exciting organ, which also happens to have the most discriminating control of all the muscular organs, being able to
distinguish gas from liquid, and liquid from solid, in its emis-
sions.

Knowledge is a form of power which has removed
the potency from, castrated, all known human qualities and
experiences. We still have human qualities and experiences,
but they have little intensity. And this is a good thing. Because if we know enough about something human to see it
from the outside, from several different points of view, then
we can get a good idea of what it looks like from the inside,
by a leap of the imagination. And then we can figure out
what its practices are in different situations, and what feelings and reactions go with what situations, from the inside.
And then, if we can see our own form of life from the outside, which we can, we can figure out what corresponds in
our practices, feelings and typical reactions, if anything, to
those of the other form of life, and use those as a starting
point to train ourselves, make ourselves, produce ourselves,
into being on the inside of the other form of life.

The thing is that if we know the back and forth movement by which our knowledge made previous types of human being what we are today, then, if it was knowledge that
made the crucial difference, we can repeat the back and forth
movement in reverse, and reproduce what was once the case.
And, since knowledge is a form of power, we can do that at
least to some degree.

But in order to get on the inside, where we take the
power of reality for granted, as obvious and natural, and not
as produced by the power of knowledge, we have to be able

to forget what we know from the outside, since that would mean not taking the knowledge for granted, which would remove its power over reality.

So first we have to get outside our own form of life, which step involves not taking the obvious for granted, and involves seeing obvious knowledge as a form of power over reality. We have to remember what we've forgotten because we took it for granted.

In order to do that, we have to get to know another culture, historical period or form of life from the outside, so that we have points of contrast from which to see our culture from the outside, alternative obviousnesses in relation to which our obviousnesses are not obvious.

Then we have to leap inside the other form of life imaginatively, to get some idea of what we're heading for. To do this we need to know a lot about the other form of life from the outside, in fact we need to know how it operates as a complete system, how all the parts which depend on each other are related. If we don't, then we're not in a position to appreciate the significance of any of the mutually dependent parts from the inside, since that significance is partly decided by the relation of the relevant part to the parts it depends on, by the precise ways it depends on them.

Since the only inside we know is that of our own culture, we'll then be really inside ours, but imaginatively inside the other. And we'll be really outside the other, but imaginatively outside ours.

Then we have to see our culture from the outside to find corresponding practices, feelings and typical reactions to give us a starting point for training and producing ourselves, points of comparison rather than points of contrast. And, similarly, to do this,we need to know how our culture works as a complete system, so that we can get sufficiently outside to register the significance of many taken for granted experiences which we don't register as worthy of attention from the inside.

41

We'll still be really inside our culture and imaginatively outside it, and we'll also still be really outside the other form of life and only imaginatively inside it.

And then we move back and forth, back and forth, until we're really inside and outside the other form of life, as well as really inside and outside ours.

And then we have to forget what we know from the outside, so that we're really inside and only imaginatively outside, which makes us really outside our own form of life and only imaginatively inside it. And then we must be prepared to complete the mourning.

We can reverse the process as well, with the inevitable mourning which is the act of really forgetting, as opposed to pretending to forget, which latter is effective as experienced by someone else relating to one from the outside, but has only the power of imagination as experienced from the inside.

This is why it's good that we have destroyed the power over reality of everything human. Because we have also destroyed the intensity of knowledge itself — we can make machines which make knowledge, it doesn't require human motivation and yearning any more, we can see the entire system of knowledge from the outside, so that we can express it completely in algorithms. And we have destroyed its power over reality by explaining it as a form of power over reality. This means that for the first time in history we can choose our knowledge, we can choose our form of reality, or at least understand how we might be able to be regarded as having done so, provided that we can forget what we know about knowledge, which means, provided that we can mourn our form of life. We can choose our disease. Knowledge itself is the only thing we cannot bring back to life, because the only thing we'll find at the end of our proofs is the choice we made or the choice some other person or system made for us to pursue the path of seeking knowledge.

This is why it was important to Voltaire, and Nietzsche, that god is dead. There is no justification for anything, no fixed point on which a demonstration of truth, a proof of knowledge, can rest, except what we choose or have chosen as the fixed point. I want to live in this way, so this is what I will agree with. I do not want to change my form of life, so that is what I will say is false, because it is false in my accepted or chosen form of life. The proof is that we *can* change our form of life, we can mourn in the service of our individual phantasies an entire value system, without being destroyed by it, and without significantly affecting the society.

This is the cultural significance of psychotherapy, which is capable of taking someone to where he or she wants to go without necessary reference to where society wants her or him to go. This is not western shamanism, if only because the one undergoing therapy is of no particular value, as an individual, to the society, and so is free to be shunned, institutionalised, and rot, if that is the choice or the way it works out.

We live in a society or culture sufficiently large and indifferent to its members for knowledge and truth not to matter. There are countless competing truths, but everyone knows all they need to know to get by, certainly all they want to know. Education is to give one a qualification for employment, not primarily a path to knowledge. And that is precisely because knowledge has won, so that there's nothing of human significance to add. Reality is taken for granted, no profoundly moving mystery, so that knowledge has nothing profoundly moving to offer. Everyone knows that you could go out and become a zen buddhist anyway, or live in Bali for a few years, so that even mysticism is profoundly banal, even mystery is unmysterious.

And it's good that we live in a culture indifferent to its members, which doesn't have to bother to dominate them because it's so taken for granted that they're dominated that that fact is forgotten. It's good because for the first time in history there's a chance not to be interfered with for some of the time, to be able to be diseased in one's own way a little of the time, between returning to the socially smoother forms of disease. Life has always been a disease. Now we can switch symptoms periodically. It's a major step in the hygienic advance of Western civilisation. Hate life, but give yourself room to scratch. This may be scrofula but it makes me laugh.

Knowledge is only in the service of life, now that it's reached its most powerful, insofar as it's forgotten. It's the only thing which can't be brought back to life, because life is hell, and to act in the light of that starting point of knowledge, which is the only life-serving impulse which could possibly motivate the restless search for something so abstracted from life as knowledge is, especially knowledge about knowledge, is to kill oneself.

The only reason to know, is so that one can choose what not to know. The only reason to acquire self-consciousness, to remember what one was already, to complete one's reality by coming to know what that reality is, to make oneself fully effective as what one is, is so that one can choose how one wishes to be unself-conscious, how one wishes to forget oneself, how one wishes to be incomplete, how one wishes to be ineffective. And all of this requires mourning, because that is how to forget, how to lose something of oneself, how to give up, so that one can forget oneself.

But this is only true at the extremes, where nothing is taken for granted, or where we can know everything including knowledge itself, so that, again, nothing can be taken for granted. Between the extremes something is already known, already a reality on the basis of which we can get somewhere and do something. The problem is what to do with knowledge at the extremes, how do you establish a power over reality which you can take for granted, which you can relax into, without landing up where you started?

If obvious knowledge was the basis of your power over reality, and you want to change your reality, and obvious knowledge was also what was stopping you from changing your reality, you have to keep obvious knowledge and lose it at the same time, remember and forget at the same time. And, since you start off in a situation in which you are where you are, and where you are is a world in which everything real is known, you can only start off changing reality by changing your knowledge, by remembering what you know so that you can change it. This means that not only do you have to remember and forget at the same time, you have to remember *in order to* forget the things that you're remembering, and forget what you know you know in order to remember what you in fact know.

You have to stop taking knowledge for granted, and you have to do so on the basis of what you take for granted about it, because it's the taking for granted which has power over reality, and that's what you need, since you want to change your reality. That means that you stop taking knowledge for granted in one area, on the basis of taking it for granted in another area. And then you find something other than knowledge to take for granted in the first area, and on the basis of that you stop taking knowledge for granted in the remaining area. And then there is no knowledge which is taken for granted, no fixed reality. But something else is taken for granted, only you can't know what that is, except by its effects. And its effects are what you just did.

So you can use knowledge to establish what the effects are, and how they relate to one another, but you can't know where you are or what you're doing. You can only know what you're doing in the known world, not what you're doing where you are. This is only true at the extremes, before you've acquired a new knowledge, which doesn't look like knowledge from the old point of view.

In a world in which everything real is obvious, any experience of a new reality will not look like knowledge, but will look obviously unreal, worthless, entertaining indulgence, unspeakable, unthinkable, impossible, culpably aberrant, contemptible. Disease. The reality of the asshole. There is no room for changing one's reality: if one does, it didn't happen, because knowledge has fixed all reality, so that if one changes to what is known, that is not real change.

To know something new about reality in a world in which all reality is obvious, is to be at the extremes. The answer is, therefore, to do what cannot be done, to think wrongly, to become what one is not, to be really unreal.

This is only the case because knowledge covers, or can in principle cover, all of reality. One response to this is to abandon knowledge altogether. But that is precisely the effect of everything's being known. If everything is known, then there is no knowledge which has a power over reality which can be experienced. Knowledge has already been abandoned, precisely because it is already everywhere. Abandoning knowledge, and committing oneself totally to knowledge, in a world in which all reality is obviously known, are the same thing. The one renounces power over the only reality there is, the other submits itself to the only reality there is, and submits itself totally because it submits itself specifically to the power which *makes* that reality what it is, a reality in which everything can be known. The one resigns itself to reality, the other helps the reality along, but both submit themselves totally to the way things are.

The only way to make qualitative change in a world in which the real is what is taken for granted as known, is to know and not know the same thing at the same time. One has to know, as something obvious, what it is that one doesn't know, so that it is real. And one has to not know it at all, so that it is different from the reality that is known. Any knowledge one produces which has power over reality will work this way anyway, for the reasons already given. And any power over reality which one may find will work this way, because all reality, in our culture, is known or knowable, is within the range of knowledge. This includes realities of which one says, "It can't be known": that's a claim to a very certain knowledge about such realities.

And, in fact, this is precisely how all knowledge in our culture already works. We know reality as something obvious, and we don't know it, because we take it so for granted that we don't register it. And that's why it's so powerful, as I've been saying. It doesn't make obvious changes, but it does keep reality powerfully stable. If you step outside it, it makes qualitative changes all the time, and keeps reality from staying the same from one day to the next.

If you abandon knowledge, you're outside, and nothing stays the same, everything is new. If you commit yourself to knowledge, you're inside, and nothing changes, nothing new happens. We're already at the extremes. And we can only move from one extreme to the other, and neither gives us any power over reality with which we can fulfil our desires or get where we, individually, want to. Unless we can play the one extreme off against the other.

It's not that there's a right way to do it and a wrong way to do it. It's that there's only one way to do it, because reality is what is known, in our culture, which means that the only way to be real is to know, and the only way to make qualitative changes in your reality is not to know, and that in turn means that the only way to have real qualitative change is to know and not to know the same thing in the same respect at the same time. Furthermore, since the taken-for-granted reality we live in or start in already works that way, *we* already work that way, and if you want to change that, then you have to know it first, which means making it real.

There's only one way to do it. And the question is what to do with knowledge. And to answer that question, you first have to find out how not to do anything with knowledge, because otherwise you've already decided. And since the extremes are here, the best way to find out how not to do anything with knowledge is to do something with complete commitment to knowledge, and then look at it from the outside. If you do something entirely without knowledge, in a world in which all reality is taken for granted as known, you'll be governed entirely by what is taken for granted, which is knowledge. That is, you have to do the opposite of what you really think should be done, in order to succeed in doing what you really think should be done. You have to go backwards in order to go forwards.

Knowledge is a form of power. As such, it operates like any form of power, only illogically. Knowledge is the only phenomenon which cannot, in principle, be explained or described logically. Anything which is not knowledge can be known from the outside, and completely described or explained by knowledge. As soon as knowledge becomes internally involved in the constitution of what it is explaining or describing, a complete explanation or description is in principle impossible within the confines of coherent knowledge, since the provision of the explanation itself changes what is being explained. Hegel thought otherwise, but Hegel was blind to his own incoherence, which was his really positive contribution to philosophy.

Knowledge is thoroughly and completely involved in its own constitution: consequently it cannot completely know itself without paradox and illogic. If it knows itself, it will be both inside and outside itself at the same time in the same respect. A description of knowledge as a form of power will therefore, if it is a complete and correct description, be inside the form of power and outside it at the same time and in the same respect. This means that it will look wrong, and if it does not look wrong, it will be incomplete or incorrect. Several incomplete descriptions or explanations can be given, however, as aphorisms, for example, which will not appear viciously illogical, since they can avoid touching on the pertinent points at which the contradictions involved oppose one another directly. They will appear as intriguing ways of putting it which could be rephrased logically and, hence, correctly. They are not. They are only correct if their illogicality is retained. That's why aphorisms bite.

In a world in which knowledge of reality is taken for granted as the only knowledge of reality, knowledge is involved in the constitution of everything real. A complete description or explanation of anything will therefore be illogical and look wrong, if it is correct. This was not the case in earlier centuries. But then knowledges of other realities were possible, as far as the life of the relevant cultures was concerned, that is, as far as the effective reality of their lives was concerned, experienced from the inside. So that knowledge itself was not taken for granted as being knowledge of the only possible reality, which meant that knowledge did not enter into the constitution of everything real. God died only in the eighteenth century, the age of rationality. Ours is the first century in which there is nothing outside knowledge. Whatever is outside knowledge is a mistake, and that is our contemporary reality which we need to take seriously, by taking mistakes seriously as the pathway to changing our realities. Newton, it is worth remembering, by way of contrast with our prejudices, was more of a theologian and alchemist than a physicist.

Knowledge is a form of power. How does the deviant, the pervert, the ambitiously creative, the childish, the inaccessibly intelligent person get her/himself recognised in such a way that the other's consciousness, knowledge of him/her will not excessively distort her/him, placing an excessively powerful binding or burden on him/her? One wants to be recognised, so that one can relate without simultaneously defending oneself against distortion far beyond what is absolutely necessary. This is not to say that one is ever unified in honesty, knowing and expressing one's true motives. But since no one is, one wants one's lies, provided that one is happy with them, to be granted the same validity as anyone else's, which includes the lies which are given validity because they are taken for granted as not being lies, but the truth about the human personality and about life in general. One wants to be allowed to mourn the truth, as everyone else has been permitted to do, to forget and take for granted that one is what one is. Particularly if what one is changes from time to time: then it is more difficult to forget alternative truths of what one is, and recognition which lets you be as far as possible is all the more necessary. One periodically abandons the power of taken for granted knowledge about oneself and life in general, and is even less able than is usually the case to defend oneself against the power of other people's taken for granted knowledge.

Another reason why it's good that knowledge has destroyed the phenomena of the human world, including itself: for the first time it is in principle possible *not* to use knowledge as a form of power, since for the first time it is evident to what degree and in what ways it is a form of power.

For the first time it is possible to recognise without oppressing, without imposing an external order: justice is in principle possible, if only on the individual level. How it is possible is not yet clear. It's the pervert's problem. Life and the human power it entails, including knowledge, is a disease in what we think of as the natural order. But to a symptom of the disease, such as a human being, disease is a good thing, provided it attacks nature in preference to attacking its own symptoms.

Socrates was right in saying that life is a disease, but he should have sacrificed Asclepius to the cock. His argument for justice in the *Republic* would have worked if he had realised that he was arguing for the bad, and not for the good. He couldn't, because it made a difference, then, what the individual did, as far as knowledge was concerned: knowledge still had to control the individual. It makes no difference now: the individual is already controlled by knowledge, is consequently of no concern to the society, and so is free to matter to her/himself and take responsibility for him/herself. Disease and morality are different words for the same thing, as Nietzsche was at pains to recognise. And Nietzsche called for a stricter morality, based on intellectual good conscience — how *much* truth can you bear, he asked — perhaps allowing, he said, for the first time, for genuine love, but, like Socrates, he made the mistake of calling that new knowledge, that new morality, health. It isn't. It's just disease turned against itself, knowledge turned against knowledge, so that it can let its other symptoms be no worse than itself.

The only new thing about our stage of civilisation is that for the first time neither knowledge nor power makes any difference except very ephemerally to oneself. And this is because we have self-knowledge, knowledge about knowledge, already, so that the only way we can improve things, the only way we can change things at all so that it matters to us, is to forget what we know, eliminate that power over ourselves. The road to advantage to ourselves lies in leaving one's penis at the door. The only way to go forwards is to go backwards, aim for fragmented power, partial knowledges.

But going backwards now is not the same as going backwards was before god died. Then, if you went backwards, you went backwards, in the wrong direction, and you went to hell or got struck by lightning or were made to drink hemlock for corrupting the youth of Athens or lost your mind and were put on display by your sister. But now that the forward, controlling movement of knowledge has won, now that it is taken for granted, so that it's part of the way things are, now if you go backwards you go forwards at the same time, anyway. So that going backwards, in comparison with what going backwards used to be, is more like not going anywhere, it's more like going sideways in relation to the path to or from the goal. For goal-oriented vision, for the eye to efficiency, it takes place just beyond the peripheries of the vision.

The thing is that once one has lost what one took for granted, it's easy to forget what one was aiming at. This only matters if one invested a lot of time, trouble and suffering in establishing just what that aim was, so that one has to go through all that again to re-establish it, and, what's more, as a consequence precisely of having taken the crucial step in getting there. It matters if one wants to enjoy one's achievement, and if one wants to choose whether to do more with it along the same or equivalent lines. The taken for granted becomes the most surprising, so that one isn't sure where it is, exactly, any more, and the surprising, which one was aiming for, becomes taken for granted, so that one isn't sure where that is any more, either. Since part of the taken for granted was that one was aiming for the new and surprising, the whole business becomes very confusing. Which pieces to put where, and why. Power, which isn't a problem any more, and knowledge about knowledge, which is.

Extremes meet and cancel one another at the point just beyond the peripheries of the goal-oriented and efficient, controlled and powerful, vision. That's when one has to deal with the fact that words don't always function the way we're accustomed to, not because they cover too little, but because they cover too much, and invade one another's space, producing a vacuum. So we need to split them and peel them off from themselves, a little at a time, so that we can follow them back or follow them through. Either way, it has to be done repeatedly, back and forth, back and forth, until we have whole words again, which we can use beyond the extremes, on either side, bracketing the extremes in the manner both of Husserl and of artillery fire, beyond the extremes, where it doesn't matter that the words are too big, because neither knowledge nor power over reality is that important beyond the extremes, and we can take the vacuums for granted, so that they're forgotten, effectively not there, as experienced from the inside.

But in the meantime you would be well advised to take some advice from your anus, which is very good at finely controlled discriminations, and is well used to dealing with imperative bits of reality that are kept out of the way.

Knowledge is a form of power. How, then, does the bad and contemptible, the pervert, criminal and insane, the eccentric, aberrantly creative and aberrantly intelligent, get her/himself recognised without having to defend him/herself simultaneously and in advance?

One way to do it is simply to present oneself and explain. That very seldom works — in fact it would be a delicious triumph of razor-keen judgment if one early and correctly assessed a case in which it would work, such cases being very exceptional — since one's presence and explanation are already marked as proceeding from a contemptible or dismissable source. In addition, prejudice is institutionalised in a person in a place that runs deeper than integrity or conscious decision. It comes from the knowledge that is taken for granted and forgotten because it is taken for granted, so that it can't be seen from the inside: the person in question might even believe beyond a shadow of doubt that s/he respects and admires the one towards whom s/he is prejudiced or whom s/he despises. S/he may actually respect and despise at the same time, and s/he need not be conscious of either. Integrity, like knowledge, is the product of training. and more integrity is the product of better training. One lands up faced with helpless hypocrisy.

So what the pervert does is this. First s/he has to get the other person to see what they take for granted. To this end s/he presents herself in terms of the other's prejudices, as sordid and strange, if not bizarre. The other then has to deal with the existence of the contemptible in a human being, so that the other has to come to terms with the fact that when they despise and reject a category, they are also despising and rejecting a human being, with human feelings. If that is of no concern to the other, then the other is beyond redemption as capable of more integrity, and a great deal of further trouble is saved.

If the other deals with his/her own destructiveness and prejudice, and is prepared to become different, s/he stops taking knowledge of the way things are for granted, and is prepared to allow surprising exceptions to the rule to be, as a source, perhaps, of new knowledge.

Then the pervert is free to be recognised in accordance with what s/he has to offer to the other person, and what s/he doesn't have to offer, and in accordance with her/his own feelings about him/herself, just like anyone else, and not in accordance with a discriminating category which comes from the realm of knowledge of reality that has been forgotten because it's taken for granted.

Then, when the bad and contemptible, the pervert and eccentric, do perverted and contemptible things, they are recognised as expressions of the pervert's personality, or as performances which are well done or badly done, and not as perverted or contemptible, except from the point of view of knowledge which is generally taken for granted, in relation to which they now function as gestures of defiance, contempt, or ridicule. Because it's only from the point of view of knowledge which is taken for granted that categories matter, make a difference to reality. Outside that knowledge they're just categories, and what matters is the attitude behind their use in any given instance.

So first the pervert capitulates to the knowledge that is already there, so that it can be acknowledged that it's really there, and so that it can be acknowledged to what extent it has power over reality. Then the pervert, if s/he has the strength, and if the other is willing, turns the knowledge back on itself — and the acknowledgement *is* the turning back on itself, which reaches completion as the acknowledgement becomes full — so that the subject of the knowledge is able or free to let him/her be whatever s/he turns out to be. The only way out is the way in. If a certain kind of knowledge is all there is, the only way to deal with it, to have any different power over reality, is to deal in terms of what there is, which is that kind of knowledge. One has to start off by doing the wrong thing, and doing it properly.

If knowledge in general, and not just a particular kind of knowledge, is all there is, the same applies: the only way out is the way in. Knowledge has to be capitulated to, consciously, deliberately, and properly, with full commitment. Until it's evident what it presupposes to operate, what it takes for granted. And then it has to be turned back on itself — the evidence has to be accepted — so that it won't interfere with what's happening, which the subject of the knowledge is then free or able to let be whatever it turns out to be, perhaps even a source of new knowledge.

And since knowledge will not necessarily play the same part in the new world of events, one may not want to get out of it in that realm at all. It may not be something one can be inside or outside, or take for granted. It may be exactly the kind of surprisingly new thing one was looking for when trying to get out of knowledge.

Since, however, one starts off inside knowledge, this means that first one has to capitulate to oneself, consciously, deliberately, and properly, at least in what one thinks and feels. Then, when one has found out what is presupposed in what one thinks and feels, what one has taken for granted so that it provides the basis on which one can spontaneously think and feel what one does, then one has to turn one's thoughts and feelings back on themselves, a turning back which is simply the honest recognition of these thoughts and feelings. Then one is free: able to choose, within the limits of one's strength, means and abilities, what one wishes to take for granted, so that one can forget about it and relax into it, and be spontaneous as whatever one trains oneself into.

And that forgetting requires the willingness to mourn, because that's how one forgets in reality and not just in imagination.

Knowledge is a form of power. But god, the ultimate explanation, is dead, so that if we want to know the workings of knowledge, we have to be necrophiliacs, desiring to penetrate within the body of a corpse, within the decaying remnants of the past, and desiring to be penetrated by the fantasied vitality of rigor mortis. If knowledge has made all of taken for granted and obvious reality what it obviously is, then we can't completely describe its workings, really, from the outside. But if we know how to get out, then we can describe the workings of knowledge at each step on the way out, as they appear on the inside. We can describe the effects of the working of knowledge completely, within knowledge itself, although we can't describe the working of knowledge independently of its effects. Since knowledge is a form of power, the effects are all we need.

The thing is that we're already on the inside of the corpse, which we take for granted, so we've forgotten, and we've taken it for granted for so long that we can turn the soggy flesh inside out through itself, at the cost of some wear and tear. But first we have to know — remember — that we live in a corpse, in the death of god, and the way to do that is to become necrophiliacs, consciously and completely. Forget the *avant-garde*. We have to remember in order to forget, remember in order to mourn and begin again.

Our commitment to the categories of the bad and contemptible, as opposed to what we on the basis of our own desires and values find bad and contemptible, is what keeps us committed to what has become bad conscience: knowledge in the place it has at bottom held throughout recorded history, the place of taken for granted power over reality, as opposed to a place which need not be oppressive, although, of course, it might be.

We need to come out at the bottom. Alternatively put, we need to let the bottom fall out, which is the same thing seen from the inside. And it must be done properly, so that it's the *bottom*, which feels, looks, smells, sounds and tastes like the bottom, otherwise the bottom still hasn't been dealt with, but still governs what is taken for granted, still connects us with what is already taken for granted. The only way to get to the top is the way to the bottom. As Heraclitus put it, the way down and the way up are the same, but the way up is better.

And you can only know after you've done it, because it occurs beyond the peripheries of the vision of knowledge which looks like knowledge. Your anus will know before you do, and you'll only know after your anus.

The pervert, the eccentric, the bad and contemptible can only be recognised if they're taken seriously. If you don't take them seriously, you're being unjust. They may want injustice, of course, but that has nothing to do with you, unless you want it to. O is proud of being a slave to men, and she already has the abuse she wants. She doesn't need it from you; but you may.

The only way to become less tight-assed is to become more tight-assed, and then to turn and catch yourself in the act. Then you can work out what you take for granted which allows you to be tight-assed without thinking about it, and then you can practise doing things which take something less tight-assed for granted, and so work through what you take for granted. Unless you like being tight-assed. Although you could always return to being tight-assed later since, if that's what you are, you're good at it.

The extremes meet, of course, so speaking through your ass is the same, but seen from the inside, as finding shit coming out of your mouth, which is what it will look like from the outside. You can't fall through the bottom without getting wet for a while, and the deeper the bottom the longer it takes to surface. One feels like sinking into the earth, and one should. It's *your* funeral, but at least it's *your* funeral.

It's also really not worth it, but if you have no choice, you might as well take yourself seriously enough to consider your individual experience as sufficiently real to be worthy of knowledge. Later, if you have something different to give you power over reality — which you will as soon as you take something, even knowledge, for granted, since from the inside it won't be experienced as knowledge, therefore won't effectively *be* knowledge, even if it *is* from the outside, because it's so taken for granted that it's forgotten — later on you can always change your mind. Is is as is does, which is not what people think it does, and consequently not what people think it is, except when they take it for granted that it is, and forget that it isn't. Then it is, and necessarily so.

It all has to do with forgetting by hiding the thing in plain sight, where it can be taken for granted, missed and mourned for without really having disappeared at all, just displaced off to the side. Not swept under the carpet, where it could be looked for: used as the carpet, so that we lift it up to look under it and — surprise — there's nothing there. So we slap the carpet back into place and give up or keep looking in the right places to look. Mind if I flick my ash on your carpet? Yes, it'll spoil the way it looks. Do you ever pay attention to it? Only when you flick your ash on it. I don't like dirt either. Yes, but this is a special occasion. We're most delicately and powerfully moved by the tangential.

Any form of knowledge which seeks to give a total explanation or account of reality, since it is a form of power, seeks to establish its power over reality as exclusive of any other power over reality. Since this power works by means of being taken for granted and forgotten, so that one can relax into it and spontaneously exercise the power of knowledge without knowing that it adds anything, without knowing that one is affecting reality, the knowledge only works as knowledge, and not as power, when it already knows, when it has already exercised its power successfully. This means that knowledge only functions as knowledge, and not as power over reality, if it is already impossible to prove it wrong, to falsify it. Truth and falsehood both find their place within knowledge; what is false is not knowledge, but that which is not knowledge, which is outside knowledge, is given its outside precisely inside knowledge. Otherwise knowledge does not give a total account of reality, does not exclude other knowledges as real powers over reality.

This also means that knowledge starts at the end, starts by having accomplished its task of knowing, and then moves backwards from there, remembering what it already knows on the basis of what it already knows, moving from piece to piece in a deepening sideways movement which produces a spiral. The last piece it finds will be the first piece, with which it succeeded in knowing but which it took for granted and forgot. That last piece will not initially look like the first piece, because it will appear as what it is when approached by knowledge, as opposed to what it is when departed from as the early starting place of knowledge. Between the beginning and the end, knowledge will know that it is going forwards, but that is because it has forgotten that it is going sideways and backwards, in a widening spiral into itself which will eventually find its boundaries.

When it finds its boundaries, it will realise that it started, once it had forgotten, in the wrong place. Because the effect of the boundaries, which were established before knowledge could knowingly begin, is necessarily to make one forget that there are boundaries at all, or to make one think of them in the wrong way, in a way which has nothing to do with what is known by the knowledge. The first step of knowledge is to make the wrong places to start look like the right places and, since there is only a choice between right and wrong, or true and false, it is also to make the right places to start look like the wrong places.

The first step of knowledge is therefore to make reality in such a way that there are right places and wrong places, true and false. One's attention cannot be specifically directed unless it can be directed at all. Consequently, whether one starts or looks in the right places or in the wrong places, one is still following the lines established by the first step of knowledge, one is still within knowledge and unable to see it from the outside.

Knowledge is therefore that which is able to put an outside inside, a form of power which is able to include what it excludes. And it does so while making the subjects of its reality take for granted that it is able to do that, so that they forget that inside covers both inside and outside, that forward covers both forward and backward, that true covers both true and false. They are then free to play true and false, inside and outside, off against one another as though they were completely independent of each other, like three dimensional objects. Until they reach the extremes, the boundaries, at which point opposing categories cancel one another and create a vacuum, because they cover too much, more than they were thought to.

This works very well, because the one thing that would remove all difficulties in removing the power over reality that is knowledge, the knowledge of the workings of knowledge itself, is the one thing that must not be known if that knowledge is to work. The only way to get it is to lose it. The only way to get all of it is to get none of it. Conversely, the only way to have none of it is to get all of it, the only way completely out is the way completely in.

The solution, the working of knowledge as seen from the outside, is hidden by being taken for granted, so that it is forgotten. That is, it is too obvious to be noticed. That means that we are already living the solution. We are already living, already knowing, on the basis of the fact that inside includes both inside and outside. This means that outside is inside of inside, which means that inside is inside and outside of inside, since inside already includes outside and inside. This means that when we say, I want to see it from the outside, what that already means is, I want to see it from the inside and from the outside. And that already means, I want to see it from the inside, since inside includes both outside and inside. And we're already doing that. That's where we are, on the inside.

The trick is that the only way to find it is by not looking for it. So that if you look for it, you won't find it. Very simple, and very effective. The first step of knowledge is to make the search for knowledge important, to make finding itself important. The first step of knowledge is to establish that something is hidden and something is found, to make us forget that what is hidden and what is found are both included in what is found. The first step of knowledge is to make the known and the unknown, and to make them in such a way that both are known: this is known, and that is unknown. When you get to the bottom of knowledge, you find something to know. You'll find a way of making one forget that two things are contained in one of these two things, making one forget in such a way that the two things become independent of each other. One thing has half of itself ripped away, and nothing changes, and there's a forgetting between.

It's not that there was originally one. It's that originally there is a ripping away of half of something, and at the same time the thing remains complete, and there's a forgetting between. And that's all. It's the forgetting that's interesting, which is why mourning is so important.

After the forgetting one still has a complete world, functioning in many independent and opposed pieces, as far as knowledge is concerned, and one has forgotten that this is unknowable, inconceivable, and consequently impossible. And then one makes spirals, shifting sideways from piece to piece, gathering up the pieces as one goes so that the spiral is more and more all encompassing, covering more of known and unknown human reality, gathering power exponentially as it moves asymptotically towards its boundaries.

The only way to break through the boundaries is to undergo a splitting into two pieces, while remaining the same, with a forgetting between. Which is what you were always doing, only now you're remembering that you're forgetting. What does that look like? It looks like this. It looks like you're slipping and sliding sideways, not getting anywhere because whenever you go forwards you find yourself back at the beginning. And that's when you're really going forwards for the first time, slnce what we think of as going forwards is really spiralling sideways, from piece to piece.

What we mean when we say, I want to go forwards, is, I want to go forwards and backwards, or sideways, because going forwards includes going backwards and going forwards. What we have a problem with, such as seeing knowledge from the outside, what we're looking for an answer to, is already solved without changing things. What we don't have a problem with — going forwards — what we're not looking for an answer to, is precisely where the answer lies, and is precisely what we have to change. There's only one way to knowledge about complete knowledge, which has complete power over reality, and this is it. You have to put it out of joint if you want to see how the joints work, and that includes putting it back into joint where it is already out of joint. Because if you're concerned with the total picture, then the total picture, the way the total picture works, is precisely by being out of joint where it already is. The existence of problems, and the existence of non-problems, are both part of the way the machine works.

The truth about truth and falsehood is that this truth is stuck to the bottom of your shoe, as Lacan puts it. Move, and it moves with you. Stop and it stops with you. Stand upside down, and it stands upside down. Do a cartwheel, and you can see the workings of the whole thing, from the inside.

But as soon as you've done the wrong thing for long enough, that becomes taken for granted, it becomes the same power over reality. So then you have to do the right thing. But that's not taken for granted any more, and you can see it as power over reality, you can watch how it works, because you're inside and outside, you're turning and catching yourself in the act all the time, remembering that you're forgetting, knowing that the carpet is under your feet because you know the carpet is under your feet, and that if you didn't know it it wouldn't be the carpet under your feet. Until you've done that for long enough, and it becomes taken for granted. Meantime you can learn to take responsibility for your power over other people's reality.

If you already know that someone else is bad, that her or his reality is not to be taken seriously, then you're sticking him or her under your shoe, you're making him or her turn and catch her/himself all the time, making her/him stand upside down, as long as you relate to her/him. Then s/he has to engage in a power struggle with you if s/he wants to be recognised so that s/he can just relax, like anyone else, into the taken for granted. You might want that. But if you relate to her/him by knowing that her/his reality is not to be taken seriously, these are the things you're doing.

All this applies only at the extremes. Knowledge is experienced as power over reality, hence is effectively power over reality, only at the extremes. Our civilisation is at the extremes. For the first time, therefore, we can take responsibility for our knowledge, for our power over reality.

Between the extremes, a between we can produce with our knowledge, that's not a responsibility which has to be taken. Then I am what I am. But if I don't like what I am, I can change it, by making use of my knowledge of the extremes. And part of my knowledge of knowledge, which arises fully only at the extremes, is that the extremes are always already here, only forgotten, pushed off to the side, where they don't matter, because they're taken for granted.

Truth about reality is always slightly elsewhere, and only slightly elsewhere, half a step behind where I am. So I have to stay where I am, take half a step back, and look, and I've got it. It doesn't matter where you start, because any starting place is wrong. And it doesn't matter where you stop, because any stopping place is wrong. All that matters is that you move by repeating the right mistakes until they're taken for granted. That's between the extremes.

At the extremes, it matters, because your life is at stake, your most valued things are at stake. And there you have to be prepared to mourn for all those things, because at the extremes you can only have it by giving it up. And what you have to mourn for is what you cherish most and what you want most. And there's nothing taken for granted to give you room to spiral from piece to piece, room to manoeuvre. There's just you, and what you want and don't have, and you have to forget it, so that you can have it and be complete. And after you've forgotten, there'll still be just you, and what you want and don't have, and you complete with what you want, and a forgetting. But then you won't be at the extremes any more, they won't be cancelling each other out so that there's a vacuum, you'll have pieces to take for granted to play with, and room to manoeuvre.

You'll still be diseased, but that will be taken for granted.

Human values: the only way to have them is to have started off by mourning them, by giving them up. The names have to be dislodged, and really dislodged, from the places in which they have so far belonged, in which they now only appear to belong. Then one can put them wherever one wants, in accordance with individual realities and emotions, or in accordance with social realities. Because the two no longer have anything necessary to do with one another. Society to-day operates according to principles that have nothing to do with individual realities, except to have power over them, in the form of categories and classes which know themselves, fully, to be categories and classes. There is justice and integrity according to society, and there is justice and integrity acording to the individual: and individual values have been completely forgotten by taking them for granted and putting them completely in the wrong place, in the hands of society at large.

And this is a good thing, because it means that individuals have been made fully real for the first time, although thoroughly degraded by their oppressive functioning in the power over reality which is society and social knowledge, so that individuals can take them up as fully real for the first time. It's all on TV, and in the media and popular books, so that one wouldn't want it. But if you mourn for it, and mourn for it properly, then you can take it up again in the right place, take it for granted in the right place, where you want it, and where it looks very different. The capacity for remembering what one wants, and for forgetting what one doesn't want, and the preparedness to do it properly, make fine discriminations very important.

Taking it for granted that a social disease is one's own virgin conception allows one to relax comfortably into it and proliferate it with exuberant spontaneity. Forgetting and mourning knowledge is forgetting and mourning all of reality, including society at large. Then one can put the pieces where one wants them. Health has always included health and disease. Disease can now, for the first time, include both disease and health: which is lucky, since it's now become clear for the first time to what degree life itself is a disease. The only way out is the way in. And all we have to do is what we've always been doing, because what we've always been doing, seeking our phantasies, is for the first time the wrong thing to do.

The point here is, firstly, that the taken-for-granted idea of health is that there is one way of being healthy which applies — even if very approximately and flexibly — to everybody, so that this taken-for-granted idea of health includes that an idea of health such as "one person's meat is another person's poison" is itself a form of disease. The taken-for-granted idea of health and normality therefore includes in advance alternative ideas or meanings of health and normality as themselves being questionable, excludable, in advance. It excludes them by including them in categories set up by itself in advance of reference to these ideas or meanings understood in their own right. The point of view within which they make sense is therefore invalidated before being heard, so that even if it *is* invalid this has not been and cannot be legitimately established.

There are many people who accept "one person's meat is another person's poison" intellectually, and who will shout it from the rooftops; but intellectual appreciation of it is neither sufficient nor of primary importance. A whole different way of living, a whole different range of attitudes, of actions, of consequences of actions which are accepted and which are repudiated, are involved in each idea of health, the taken-for-granted idea and the idea that the taken-for-granted idea is valid for some while what the taken-for-granted idea correctly means by disease may validly be health for others. Because of the extensive life-concerns involved, what is primarily important is a slow training of character.

The point here is, secondly, that all of this is true only from the point of view of the idea which is not taken-for-granted, since *all* of this is invalidated in advance by taken-for-granted knowledge, as some form of disease: excessive idealism, cynicism, masturbatory word-play, the indulgence of various unsavoury motives. And this invalidation is correct: certainly by the criteria of taken-for-granted knowledge, and also by the criteria of the other point of view, for which taken-for-granted knowledge is given its basic criteria by serving the purpose of domination without taking responsibility for that domination, which purpose it serves perfectly consistently.

And the point here is, thirdly, that the point of view which is not taken-for-granted is not necessarily reached only by complete absence of the taken-for-granted viewpoint. It *is* radically and completely different from that viewpoint; but this difference includes a knowledge, with its implied ways of living and feeling, that radical and complete difference can involve having *both* points of view *simultaneously*, in a certain kind or kinds of way. Thus disease includes both dis-ease and health.

All of this is of course so far expressed in the terms of taken-for-granted knowledge. The whole thing has to be re-thought and re-articulated if it is to be expressed from the point of view of the other kind of knowledge, without refer-ence to the concerns of taken-for-granted knowledge. One would have to *start* one's thinking in terms, for example, of *winning through*, and *fighting for*, as opposed to winning where someone loses as being of primary importance, instead of thinking so as to *reach* ideas like that of winning through as being primary.

In fact, one of the things one wins through and fights for *is* the overcoming of the circumstances of caring about winning and losing. In *Utopia*, More writes, "No town has the slightest wish to extend its boundaries, for they don't regard their land as property but as soil that they've got to cultivate."[1] There, there is no need to fight for the right to one's and everyone's place in the scheme of things. The pres-ent account would then be meaningful perhaps only in rais-ing children, and in exceptional circumstances to be involved in which would be one of the epiphanic privileges life some-times affords. (This is not the way More puts it; but it is, perhaps, the way his friend Erasmus does, in *The Praise of Folly*.)

But the present account is concerned to do justice to taken-for-granted knowledge, for the sake, of course, of *both* sides, since the knowledge which is not taken for granted be-comes taken for granted by those who live in accordance with it. I believe that a great deal of what is taken simply to be irony in Plato's Socrates, in Marx, in Nietzsche and in Freud, is in fact also sympathetic and fully affirming. Marx in particular was quite explicit about this.

In fact, the point emphasized throughout this book is that the idea is also to defend *the opposition* from their *own* taken-for-granted knowledge. They're not experienced in questioning basic categories, certainly not in more than a purely theoretical or hypothetical way, so that, should one defend oneself successfully, in a way they notice, against the oppressive force of their taken-for-granted categories, without their more than half understanding one's own point of view, they are likely to judge their own failure oppressively in terms of those still taken-for-granted categories. This is what, as I see it, Gandhi did. It's just, it's perfectly fair, but it's most unpleasant, it doesn't fulfill one's desire to make the world, in whatever little way one can, a better place to live in, and it hurts oneself, since one is standing by in the presence of an oppressive act.

It's unfair to ask one *not* to stand by, since one has after all in effect been attacked, and is merely defending oneself. But one has here an opportunity to force one's own principles of non-oppression, of defending the other point of view as well as one's own, on the opposition, to fight fairly for this principle of one's own position, and, since at this point *both* points of view are fully in the picture, one's intervention in thinking this opportunity is both an act of love *and* one of aggression. If the opposition remains more than half unrecognising of one's own position, the act disappears entirely for them, since it has meaning only where one's point of view remains in the picture, which it ceases to do if it remains unrecognised except to the extent to which one forces it to be further recognised. If they come to recognise one's position properly, then one's act has been a friendly and helpful act, since, because of it, they don't condemn themselves so harshly. Prior to either outcome, one's defending them against themselves is as loving as it is aggressive, and so makes no difference to one's defending oneself; it costs one nothing in the long run, beyond a minor cause of added resentment for which one has cause enough not to worry about a little more or a little less.

The *fact that* one bothers *at all*, however, is one's contribution to making the world a pleasanter place to be in, and the fact that it may be ineffective is one's guarantee that it *is* such a contribution, and not an oppressive imposition of one's own values and understanding of things.

So, in order to defend the opposition from their own taken-for-granted knowledge, in the process of defending *oneself* against it, one goes along with not being fairly taken into account or recognised, which will in any event happen whether one goes aong with it or not: one accepts their point of view, for which one's own does not exist. then one treats them in the way they've been treating one: one entirely ignores the existence of their point of view; but one does so in the way a non-oppressive person does, only in self-defence against their preceding attitudes and actions, not as a gratuitous act of violence. In this way one shows them how to behave toward themselves, towards their own history of taking for granted. This has no meaning for them, and will only acquire meaning for them if their imposition of their values and understanding of things fails in a way they notice. This is one's contribution to non-oppression, one's defence of them. One shows respect for their principle, by being prepared to use it, and one shows them in their terms how to respect one's own principle, by being prepared to take responsibility for following theirs. And if one does so resentfully and vengefully, one is usually being even more supportive to them, if somewhat unkind to oneself.

Thirdly, one returns to one's way of doing things: either dismissing their impositions on one while recognising the validity of their understanding and values for themselves; or avoiding significant contact with them altogether, having made one's contribution towards making the situation one which can become pleasant, should one feel unwilling to remain significantly involved in a situation in which what one values is consistently being overridden, and in which one is making all the effort towards having a two-way relationship.

To do all this requires none of this articulation and no

thought-out decisions as to when to do what. It requires only genuine caring and honesty. If one does not care and is not concerned to do anything requiring honesty, then the genuinely caring and honest thing to do is to accept the consequences of not caring and being dishonest: if, under those circumstances, one understands and accepts not being treated as a caring and honest person, then one is being genuinely caring and honest, for who one is, and this whole account in fact applies, perhaps with an extra touch of admirability.

All of this account is merely an articulation of what one already finds oneself aiming towards doing if one is a genuinely caring as well as an honest person, as I understand this to the extent of my honesty.

One may not succeed in doing this; one may have other, more pressing, concerns; one may prefer to avoid complexities altogether. But I think this is an accurate account of what would feel most right in situations where one *has* become involved in oppression by taken-for-granted knowledge, if one is genuinely caring and honest, or an accurate account of what is involved in one's feelings if one is simply too exasperated to do anything but be exasperated.

And, to quote Wittgenstein, perhaps pertinently,

> There may be strong prejudices against uncovering something nasty, but sometimes it is infinitely more *attractive* than it is repulsive. Unless you think *very* clearly psycho-analysis [for example] is a dangerous & a foul practice, & it's done no end of harm &, comparatively, very little good. (If you think I'm an old spinster — think again!)[2]

The point of all this, finally, is that to be honest about what one takes for granted, and to accept the consequences of living it out, *is* to live in accordance with the non-taken-for-granted point of view, *whatever* one takes for granted, including the idea of health as one thing applicable universally to all. One's knowledge is then simply knowledge, not a form of power, because that knowledge does not then play a part in coercion: it can be challenged as *knowledge*, by points of view not delegitimated in advance, and the use of force is then clearly the use of force, for which the user is clearly responsible.

It doesn't matter, then, which terms one uses to express all this, as long as it is remembered that two sets of meanings and attitudes are involved in each of the basic ideas. This whole account so far has been an attempt to show how this confusion of two sets of meanings can be necessary and helpful, and to follow and articulate the process by which this confusion is necessary and helpful, when it is.

And one has to follow the process, if one is following it in any way, with oneself, and not only with others. The difference between the two points of view and ways of life lies simply in that in the one, the end is a different place that one reaches, abandoning the process of getting there, while in the other, the different place *is* the willingness to follow that process, slowly to train one's character, and the attitude and understanding which go along with appreciation of the nature of this process, when one's taken-for-granted knowledge, *whatever* it may be, including the *non*-taken-for-granted point of view, may not fit with what one finds. One cannot know in advance, not only that one's taken-for-granted knowledge is correct, but also that it's *in*correct. In fairness to both sides, and for the sake of genuine knowledge or truth, one can only follow the process of being confused between two knowledges, one of which one does not know if one knows, and one of which one knows one does not know.

Even if one intends to change who one is, one has to be who one is, thoroughly, in order to make the change genuinely a change of *who one is* to being different. And in order to be who one is, to be honest, one has to pursue this process, since honesty begins by acknowledging that it's not easy to know one's motives and reliable or enduring and unreliable or equivocal traits. One is again in a position of beginning with a taken-for-granted knowledge, which may or may not be true, and having to treat that knowledge in such a way as to allow for the recognition of a different understanding, the nature of which is still to be made clear on the basis of one's treatment of one's taken-for-granted knowledge. There is nowhere to start but where one is; but starting where one is is what allows one to get somewhere else. A pointlessly unilluminating statement when it comes to places, but not so pointless when it comes to orienting oneself in the conduct of one's life.

It works like this. Inside includes inside and outside. Health includes health and disease. Outside is inside of inside. Disease is inside of health. Outside is inside of inside and outside of inside, because inside includes outside and inside. Therefore disease is inside and outside of health. Inside including outside is not, however, symmetrical with outside being inside of inside as well as outside of it, since inside does not include outside by being inside it, which is how outside excludes inside or how it would have to be said to include it. Disease being inside and outside health is therefore not symmetrical with health including disease. We haven't managed to reach legitimately a position in which disease can be said to include health in a way which is symmetrical with the implications which flow from the statement that health includes disease. Outside includes outside and excludes inside in such a way that it is inside inside. Disease includes disease and excludes health in such a way that it is inside health. Disease is still covered by health.

At the extremes inside and outside, health and disease cancel one another out, producing a vacuum or gap. On the way back from the extremes you can run it back to where you started, or you can switch over. Our culture has reached the extremes: the contemptible is admirable or to be feared,

72

and *Star Trek* is good precisely because it's so bad.

Switching, if you run it backwards from the end where one starts to the beginning, it looks like this: health being inside and outside disease is not symmetrical with disease including health. Health is inside and outside disease. Disease includes disease and health. The directionality of the places previously belonging to the conjunctions, prepositions and the sequencing of statements which they condition is still with us and disrupts the continuity of the flow of meaning in repeated jarring breaks.

Running it forwards, that is, in the way it looks simply from the inside, it looks like this. Disease includes disease and health. Health is inside disease. Therefore, according to the logic of inside and outside, health is inside and outside disease. But this is not symmetrical with disease including health: health includes health and excludes disease in such a way that it is inside disease.

A dead end either way, which, away from the extremes, allows a taking for granted that the other reality will not intervene. In the gap, only one of the two pairs of opposites is switched, otherwise you're back to where you started. At the extremes, every term coincides with its opposite, so every one thing is in fact already two. That's why, thinking about it conversely, one needs two pairs of opposites to have two things.

Away from the extremes, the presence of the opposite of what is being said is pushed off to the side, where it isn't noticed. Rightly so, since it's only relevant if one's making a statement about the nature of reality which intends to exercise power over reality. This is not the intention away from the extremes, since reality is already taken for granted there; statements about it are really statements about knowledge, or expressions of emotion. Everything is determined: that says, now you can't hold me responsible for anything. The world is made of atoms: that says, we know how to make a bomb and are impressed by it.

The old knowledge and the new knowledge are the same thing fitting snugly head to toe with its double, and with half of itself switched round while the other half remains constant. Since it's upside down in relation to its double, it's also laterally inverted as it first appears, but it's laterally the same seen upside down, which is to say, seen from the inside. Or, it's the same way up when it's not seen laterally inverted, which is also from the inside. Either way, half of it is still switched round and half of it remains the same. Exactly what is switched round and exactly what is the same depends entirely on which oppositions are basic to one's subject matter at the time, which of course depends entirely upon one's subject matter. One could keep inside and outside the same and switch health and disease, or vice-versa, depending on one's concern, or one could keep now and then constant in order to switch here and there, or vice-versa, and so on.

Knowledge is a form of power. When faced with taken-for-granted knowledge which is total knowledge, how does the pervert get her/himself to be recognised without being unfairly oppressed? The only way, when faced with total conviction, is to concede that you've lost, that your position is already held within that of the opposition. Then you go sideways inside the opposition's territory until you reach a dead end. Then you turn around with the opposition, catching yourselves in the act of both having gone sideways. Then you switch places with the opposition. And you go sideways in the opposite direction, so that your pieces are there but they don't yet make sense, which they can't, given that it's a new sense, at least for the opposition, and also for you, insofar as you're now occupying the opposition's position: the pieces can't yet make sense until they're all there — knowledge only starts once it's already succeeded in establishing what is to be known. In fact the opposition might only get to the point at which they can realise that the pieces don't make sense as they presently appear once they've reached the end of this second reversed sideways movement. Then you turn around, switching positions with the opposition again, when you've reached the end of that second movement, which end is your own starting point — disease includes disease and health — and you go sideways in the original direction, until you reach your own dead end. And then the opposition is in your territory.

Then you've both been in both territories, and you can both hang upside down from the ceiling and talk to each other, instead of just one of you having to do it all the time. The territories — and knowledge — have become a matter of choice, and not of power over reality which includes the other person's reality. Conversation can happen instead of power struggle, each with power over her/his own reality.

From the point of view of taken-for-granted knowledge, there are four movements: the first sideways movement, which is paradoxical but legitimate: then the third one, implicitly, which is illegitimate in the terms of the knowledge with which one began, and which permits the articulation of the second movement; then the second movement, which is only possible, only makes sense, on the implicit basis of the third, being nothing but that third movement backwards; and then the third movement, explicitly. From the perverted point of view, there are only three steps, but the place occupied, from the other point of view, by the slid-under third movement, is occupied by the gap of mourning.

Consequently, from the straight point of view the order is one, three, two, three. But then three has become four, and two has become three, so it's one, four, three, four. And so on, until a complete circle has been described and we're back at one shifted over to the side, one, ten, nine, ten. Then we start again, 10, 12, 11, 12. This is the meaning of Hegel.

The second movement, in illegitimate reversed sideways movement, is constituted by an oscillation, a bracketing swing, which accompanies the second movement as it shifts it along, but oscillates more and more widely with respect to the first movement. Clearly, this gets nowhere, because its accomplishing anything automatically means that it has to go somewhere else. But eventually it covers everything, or enough to be taken for granted, and then there's nothing for it but to mourn where one was. And that means mourning legitimacy, mourning going straight. And that means that the third step or movement can meaningfully be regarded as legitimate, since what one wants becomes the starting point for establishing a knowledge, a taken for granted, as Edmund so clearly sees in *King Lear*. So that the second step is legitimate, if confused, and the third step doesn't need to be slid back under the second. And then what used to be going sideways and getting nowhere is going forwards and getting somewhere.

The order is now, one, oops, two, oh my what's happening, three. And this is the meaning of Wittgenstein.

This process applies only at or around the extremes, where it's evident that knowledge is a form of power and not forgotten by being taken for granted. I have said that we need do nothing different from what we've already been doing in order to follow this process, since our society is already at the extremes or around them and so is already turning itself inside out, like a glove. But this statement comes from a body of knowledge which does not take the extremes for granted, and is addressed to a body of knowledge which does. That means that, in order not to have to change, you have to be in a different place, you have to change for it to be the case that you don't have to change.

So the first step involves acquiring knowledge about what you're doing and taking for granted, and then you're already moving sideways, along the surface of what you're also already doing, which means that, to keep going in the new direction, you must keep doing what you were doing in the old direction, while acquiring knowledge about it. Then, to change directions, you have to take for granted what you're doing again, that is, you have to not know again, which happens by sheer repetition, so you don't have to do a thing except to keep going in the same direction. Then, to change directions after this, you have to acquire knowledge about what you're doing, because you only change by not changing when you're at the extremes, and now that you're taking the extremes for granted, you've forgotten and aren't there any more. Conditions for change switch back and forth as one changes one's relation to taken for granted knowledge, which is what we call nature or reality.

Of course, the only way not to know, at the extremes, is by knowing, and we could interpose that step and its consequences between the first and second steps or movements, instead of covering it under the heading of repetition, and then we would have perpetual oscillation heading nowhere.

That doesn't matter. As long as we arbitrarily stop interposing the step between the first and second somewhere, and settle for a gap in legitimate knowledge. Then we can follow through, go sideways for a long enough period of time to forget the absence of the step between the first and second steps. This has affinities with the reasoning involved in infinitesimal calculus.

The closer we are to the extremes, the harder it is to forget that absence for a long period of time, because the less there is of a taken for granted to relax into. And the closer we are to the extremes, the longer the necessary period of time is, because the more there is of a taken for granted still to cover and establish. That's where the capacity to mourn comes in, as where one is and what one wants are torn apart with increasingly lingering violence and increasingly violent slowness.

At the extremes, where urgency and patience, speed and slowness, succession and simultaneity, are most at odds, most immediately implied and bound up each in the other, and each independently most crucial and valued, one step after another desperately requiring and at the same time desperately opposed to all the steps at once, the measures of time decide the measures of the switches of direction, and not the decimal measures of our less archaic, less primitive, number system. Thus the switching over to the side which occurs after the sequence one, ten, nine, ten is replaced by an occurrence after one, twelve, eleven, twelve, and multiples of five of twelve, and multiples of twelve of that. That is, at the extremes, it takes longer than you would expect, and it's all rather approximate.

But what you come out with is, first, six of one and half a dozen of the other; then, half a dozen of one and six of the other; and then six of one and half a dozen of the other, and you're out of the extremes again, going forwards and taking it for granted, so that you can forget that going forwards is, at bottom, going sideways, or, alternatively, has a hole in it.

That gap, where the third step slides implicitly under the second to go before it, is the necessity imposed on reality by taken for granted knowledge, or consciousness. Consciousness is a flaw in the world, an act of disjointed rippling which throws everything in the world, including itself, agonisingly out of joint. When Hamlet says, the time is out of joint, o cursed spite that ever I was born to set it right, he only has that problem because he notices.

He only has a problem knowing what to do because he asks questions, because he wants to know why it's necessary to have to do anything, why things are wrong. But to answer these questions he would have to go back before the beginning, to find a place which isn't already the wrong place to start, because the whole of Denmark, unfortunately, is in a rotten state and not vice-versa. The only way to know is to start off by not knowing, the only way to recover his values is to sacrifice them, take the poison. That meant death, then, because the individual still mattered to society at the beginning of capitalism, so their values were intertwined. As with Socrates.

Today the individual doesn't matter to society, is taken for granted and forgotten, made irrelevant by being too obviously important. So the two sets of values have nothing to do with one another. We don't notice now, as Hamlet noticed, not because we are more aware of alternatives or more sophisticated than he, but because we have even less sense of reality than he did: we've forgotten what it feels like when things are wrong, because disjointedness itself has been forgotten by being taken for granted. The death of values now appears to be the life of values.

As on *Star Trek*. The prime directive is, do not interfere with the lives of other species; but something is always already wrong when contact is made. And the only way to put it right, to deal justly, to obey the prime directive, is to interfere and betray the prime directive. And there's always a mourning, and always the next episode. To sleep, perchance to dream, and always the morning after.

As Heraclitus put it, near the beginning of our civilization, awake, all he sees is death; asleep, dreams. The place of life in knowledge is neither here nor there. This was not the problem. This was the solution to the problem of the relation of knowledge to life, the place of life in knowledge. A problem which contained in itself its own solution. Now, around the end of our civilisation, the problem is that the place of life in knowledge is neither here nor there. And the solution is the relation of knowledge to life, the place of life in knowledge. Life, then, was bigger than knowledge. Now, knowledge is larger than life.

Now we have a solution which contains in itself its own problem. If we were to express this transposed state of affairs in the thought that ran from Heraclitus to Hegel, it would read, at bottom, the placing of life in knowledge is neither now nor then. Away from the extremes, however, oscillation and the twistings of related and opposed oppositions are taken for granted, forgotten, do not occur, therefore, and can be detected only in the gradual movement of long periods of discourse, and not within the elements of the words and sentences themselves.

This is the meaning of Kant, and all that follows him. In Hegel it's hardest to see because it's too obvious; knowledge of knowledge, knowledge which can manage its own boundaries, is only arrived at in the perpetual movement from one mistaken position of knowledge to another mistaken position of knowledge, and when all the mistakes have been made and made properly, as experienced from the inside. In Kant the dislocations, the points of breakdown which necessitate a swing to another angle of approach, are evident. I am but mad north-north-west. When the wind is southerly, I know a hawk from a hansaw.

Since then we've been oscillating between Kant and Hegel, between architectonic autocritique which aims at a dead end, and spherical system in perpetual movement. Marx and Nietzsche mark the switch of position which begins the second sideways movement after this first step into the oscillation. And Freud and Lacan mark the switch of positions which allows the third sideways movement back again, to a dead end which includes, if it wants, the spherical perpetual movement, instead of vice-versa.

So now, for the first time, we can go forwards, or sideways in the context of going forwards, instead of going forwards, or forwards in the context of going sideways. Or vice-versa; but for the first time we have a choice.

What is justice? The answer is given in the first book of Plato's *Republic*. Justice, in the context of naive consideration for others, is giving each person her or his due. Justice, in the context of perceptive knowledge of the way things are, is the right of the stronger. Socrates refutes both of these answers in book one, the second taking up the remaining nine books of the dialogue as well. He refutes the second, however, on the basis of the first which he has already refuted: this is clear from his insistence that each part of the soul or state is ordered in accord with justice only when its own concerns are best accommodated, that is, when each part is given its due. He states this the other way round, because he approaches it in reverse: it's not enough to say that justice is giving each his or her due: due must be given from her/his own point of view, and that requires going backwards as well as forwards.

Socrates lets everything hang from the highest good. But that is not his concern — his concern is justice. And what he wants to do, from his position, is to be given his due as a story teller. The last part of book ten of the *Republic* is a myth, a story, told by Socrates in monologue, after he has refuted, like a wrestler, the claim that justice is the right of the stronger, for the third time. And the *Timaeus*, consisting in two monologues, is, according to Socrates, the telling of myths without which the *Republic* is a still-life, not moving as living creatures do.

The problem is that, if one is to give someone else her/his due, one has to be prepared to work according to his/her highest good as well as according to one's own. And the only way to do that is to go backwards and forwards, to betray both highest goods in order to fulfil them, since one is working at the boundaries, at the extremes, of the points of view which flow from these different values or priorities. Each point of view has to start before its own beginning in order to do justice to the different and perhaps unrelated starting point or grounding values of the other, in order not to begin by imposing its values on the other even before communication begins.

Socrates does this. He defeats the second position by a display of rhetorical power, thus fulfilling the condition that justice is the right of the stronger. And he gets to tell his story for nine books, in the terms in which his values can be appreciated by the opposition, and for the last book in his own terms: in which everyone gets their due after death, and before the next beginning, according to the goods they've chosen. Backwards in three wrestling movements and then forwards. And he defeats the first position in book one by showing its naivety, thus giving it its due as its due would naively appear: then he ties this refuted position supportively into the remainder of his argument, so as to give it its due from the point of view of his good, which is to tell sophisticated stories and to be just in accordance with sophisticated intelligence, which knows how to give all the goods their due from their own point of view.

He gives Polemarchus his due in book one, in a way Polemarchus can't appreciate, and himself his due in book ten, in a way Polemarchus can appreciate; and he gives Thrasymachus far more than his due for nine books during which he gives him nothing he can appreciate. A masterly and slavish handling of the problem of knowledge and power at the extremes.

This can only be done when the extremes are not taken for granted and forgotten. When they are, going forwards is going forwards, going backwards is going backwards, and never the twain shall meet. When the extremes are taken for granted, there is only the naive view, and the perceptively knowing view, and these can only be opposed to and exclusive of each other; the dialogue moves sideways between them, never getting anywhere, because away from the extremes the position of knowledge is taken for granted, one can't be inside it and outside it at the same time.

This is why Socrates has to argue in terms of one highest good, and one only: Thrasymachus would regard anything less power-hungry as contemptibly unreal. In the *Timaeus* Socrates asks for stories to bring the *Republic* to life; in the *Republic* he forbids poetic stories in the light of the sole highest good: not his highest good; Thrasymachus', the one who is committed to knowledge of the way things are, as opposed to naive stories, like giving everyone their due. Thrasymachus' truth was, for Socrates, just another story. And he could tell stories in Thrasymachus' truth-terms better than Thrasymachus could tell the truth in Socrates' stories.

Thrasymachus was obviously stronger, and he still didn't win. And Socrates didn't win or lose, since he was proving Thrasymachus right in order to prove him wrong: he just got to tell one of the most sophisticated stories ever told. He looped out sideways, via Thrasymachus' taken-for-granted knowledge, which presupposes taken-for-granted values, a taken-for-granted highest good, which constitutes reality for everyone, from Thrasymachus' point of view, and not just for himself. How to be recognised in the face of taken-for-granted truth? Give up, go sideways, reverse sideways on an illegitimate premise, return sideways for the third time, and then you can tell your story. On the morning after, perhaps Critias and Timaeus will feed you with their stories, and you can be free to use your ass for sitting on. But make sure you can go without nourishment for a long time, because you might have to wait through many mornings before anyone finds out where you are.

Meantime, away from the extremes, stories are just stories, truth is truth, and if your highest good is not generally known to be a good then it's worthless. Hence Socrates is despised by the older generation for his naive and contemptible foolishness, and he's despised by the rest of history, as can be seen in the condescending reverence for his lovable, childlike goodness of heart. He is respected because he's so easy to patronise without knowing it. He didn't just tell stories. He told *the* stories. In his time, he was regarded as one who just told stories, because *the* wasn't possible any more. In subsequent history he was regarded as telling *the*, because stories stopped being stories, having become irrelevant. Then, he was despised for being impossible; later he was despised for being too possible. But he told *the* stories, for which he said you must know nothing, and you must have examined your life, and you must have integrity, which requires all the virtues — virtue being *arete*, excellence —including wisdom.

To appreciate — recognise — Socrates, you first have to know that he was telling stories, and then you have to know that he wasn't just telling stories. If you know that he wasn't just telling stories flrst, you're wrong, you've missed Socrates. Unless you're Plato, in which case you can hide behind Socrates, and make it clear to people that you're telling stories before they try to find what it is that you're not *just* doing with your stories; unless they're too stupid to see the obvious, which they usually are.

At bottom, Socrates was too smart for his own good. On the other hand, he was seventy before they gave him the hemlock, bad as he was in their eyes. And all we know about him is his name, good as he was in our eyes. If you can't help being drafted, all you can do is keep your head down and not volunteer for anything. And the stories were the point, anyway. Maybe after you're dead Homer will talk to you. *He* wasn't interested in fighting battles; and the other people there, who came from Homer's mouth or pen, are already dead anyway, and perhaps will have time enough to listen, and the excellence to listen well.

In our time there's really nothing at stake, and no excuse for injustice on the individual level beyond a failure to examine one's life and follow through, which latter requires courage, forbearance, and the love of knowledge and justice, as one swings sideways around the gap created in one's own goods by the presence of other people's taken-for-granted goods.

This isn't me, folks, says Socrates, I know nothing. Part of what I know is that you don't know anything either. And I'm trying to tell you that's nothing. There's a lot more than that to knowing nothing. Take Alcibiades, for instance. There's nothing at stake. I know nothing. I'm a lot of fun to be with. Take Alcibiades for instance. There's a lot more than that to knowing nothing. And I'm trying to tell you that's

nothing. Part of what I know is that you don't know anything. I don't know anything. This isn't me, folks.

Yes, Socrates. Have some hemlock. Plato's sick. I think
he just learnt something.

Nietzsche wrote a book to ensure that he would be
recognised, *Ecce Homo.* In it he says that he would much
rather not do this — as elsewhere he says that what he likes
about Socrates is, above all, what he did *not* say — but he
wants to make sure that, above all, he is not mistaken for
anyone else. In the book he describes his rather sordid family background, insisting that he was of noble Polish stock,
which he wasn't, but he *was* flamboyantly absurd and terribly sentimental, and he tells you how strong he likes his tea,
and at what hours he likes to have it, and he tells you about
his books. He also tells you how subtle and complicated he
is, and that *Thus Spoke Zarathustra* does not have a loud note
in it, i.e., he is not Wagner. And the chapter headings, "Why
I am So Wise," "Why I am a Destiny," etc., are presumably
not to be read in Wagnerian. So when he says, I am dynamite, he presumably did not mean that he had a constitution
like an ox, or a tuba. He probably meant that he was one of
the first people in history who knew what s/he was doing,
and that that was quite a thing.

Beyond good and evil. First there were good people,
leisurely and gracious inside the community, lawless and
savage out of it, as opposed to the bad, who were contemptible because they worked, and not to be noticed because that
was the way things were. The gods said so, or the ancestors
did, or the way things were did. Then this was turned upside down, the good stopped being the evaluators who
counted, who had social salience, and the bad became the
evaluators. So there were — and are — evil people, the formerly good and noble, now lawless and savage inside the
community, jittery and ungracious outside it, people who do
not work and who must be noticed at all costs so that they

can be forgiven and redeemed, i.e. made to work. God said so, or the constitution did. And there are good people, the formerly bad and contemptible, who work, who are lovingly lawless and savage inside the community, and politely jittery and ungracious outside it. The good people are repressed, they've turned their instincts back on themselves, and the evil people are not repressed, but exceedingly uncomfortable.

Guess which Nietzsche was? Well, his instincts had been turned back on themselves, at the end of the good/evil illness, an illness, he says, in the sense in which pregnancy is an illness. And he wasn't repressed, but he was exceedingly uncomfortable. And he thought maybe genuine love was possible for the first time. And he knew that Christianity was responsible for the fibrillated delicacy, the richly decadent rot and mould, the Camembert-like over-ripeness, that is high culture. And he didn't like anti-Semites. And he thought maybe punishment of the stranger could become obsolete, and that that would be a wonderful thing. And he wanted very badly to be noticed, and was prepared to work for it, even though that was the way things were. And he was leisurely and gracious outside his non-existent community, and jittery and ungracious in his books, inside it. He was all confused.

God was dead. A crime for which everyone was responsible, so that everyone was a criminal, and no one, therefore, could any longer be singled out as a criminal. Society as a whole had transgressed its boundaries, gnawed through the roots of its own values. There was no longer anything fundamental, nothing the removal of which was unthinkable; there was, therefore, no longer anything fundamentally at stake for the society as a whole. Anything, fundamentally, mattered as much or as little as anything else. Neither god's word nor that of the law, at bottom, mattered.

God was dead, and community was dead, replaced by a collection of individuals with no value or set of values to celebrate in common or sacrifice to in common. And consequently knowledge, as it had been, was dead, since, with nothing ultimately at stake, it could have no universal, no communally binding, significance. Including the knowledge that god, community and knowledge were dead. The only one it mattered to was Nietzsche. And so he had to place the attitudes that went with the old values where they really counted for him, because that was the most he was going to get out of them, and they really did matter to him.

Like Socrates, he could only hope that someone would listen, and see him; there was no way he could directly show himself to a community which knew, with a knowledge of the obvious, that it was still alive, for which *he* was the one, as he suggests in *Ecce Homo*, who was dead, obviously unreal. But unlike Socrates, there was no one at all for him to talk to who was in a position to take him seriously and thereby confirm that he was at least *dealing* with something real, even if he himself wasn't yet in a position to specify exactly what this different reality was, so that he could safely abandon the crippling urgency of the need to prove and be certain until he had advanced far enough on his road to be sure about exactly what it was that he was defending, and relax into that simplicity. No one to talk to, pederasty being out of the question by the nineteenth century. He was never in a position to be recognised, so that he could learn how to speak forwards for anyone other than imaginary interlocutors. He was never in a position, when expounding his thought, to be anywhere but the extremes; and with no knowledge to take for granted, he could never relax, because he could never be sure he wasn't in the opposition's territory. Perverts had a harder time in those days, too. Hence he tells us, at the end of his creative life, that he likes strong tea, and at what hours of the day, at the same time as telling us that he is a destiny.

Meantime, the question was where to put the values. And the line that begins the *Genealogy of Morals* is, We do not know ourselves, we men of knowledge. How could we, Nietzsche says, we have always been searching elsewhere, far and wide, like bees in search of pollen. The honours and the shames belong to the one who knows, the glory finds its place, now, in the inglorious. The contemptible ones, the dealers in words and not in deeds, the people, if you like, of the book, the ones who keep away from social power and the recognition of social esteem, these are the only ones in a position to bestow honours, to revaluate values, to decide where contempt should go. Because these are the only ones who know that we no longer know. And these are the only ones who are in a position to exercise and therefore rightfully claim the excellence, the virtues, required to follow through with that knowledge; success in the social realm, after all, now requires anything but excellence and integrity.

The individual's world is now where life lies, as far as notable or admirable striving is concerned, and this fact is the one thing that the creative have in common, the one piece of knowledge which is of common import to them, and which it is pressing on all of them to deal with, and to give due regard to its tremendous implications, its enormity. This is how I like my tea. I am a destiny. Pass the sugar, please. This is a courage, a temperance, a justice, a wisdom, the virtues of acquiring knowledge about knowledge, which have never, since Socrates at least, had a real importance. Now they do. It's time for the bad, the contemptible, the evil, the pervert, the patronised, the artist, to stand up and evaluate themselves otherwise, because they can, now. God, the clumsy guarantee of the single and unsubtle vision, is dead. And they have done so, most strongly and publicly since the 1960's.

And many of them have made the same mistake as Nietzsche. They took the disease as an illness in the sense in which pregnancy is an illness. They forgot where they were coming from, what their aim was, and what they had learned while they were there. Like Nietzsche, they moved sideways in the opposition's territory, finding that what was called symmetry included an asymmetry; then they switched and went sideways in reverse, calling for civil rights and recognition; but, like Nietzsche, they failed to switch positions and return again. This means that they were indeed out of the opposition's territory, but that all that they had to relax into was their own taken-for-granted run backwards, so that it didn't make sense yet, it didn't have the same power over reality. They hadn't reached their own dead end as it would appear in being approached from their own forward direction; they hadn't reached their own taken-for-granted away from the extremes where they could be recognised in any simple, relaxed, non-self-cancelling, non-oscillating way.

This means that they got out of the opposition's taken-for-granted knowledge, only in order to drop back into it when they wanted to relax and be recognised. They changed the material conditions of their oppression to a marked degree, but failed to change the knowledge that went with the original material conditions. That is, they changed themselves as much as they changed the opposition, for the sole purpose of dealing with the opposition, and, having succeeded in that dealing to a large degree on the material level, they forgot and failed to return to their own position to be recognised in the way that they originally aimed to be, an aim which motivated their getting to the partially successful place in which they proceeded to forget why they got there in the precise detail of that why. Homosexuals tend to disapprove of flaming queers, and go for the macho, brutal, or conservative. Feminists disapprove of cosmetics on women and of female indirectness and manipulativeness. Blacks disapprove of blacks who have rhythm. Because God or the constitution or Marx said so. But God is dead, and so is Marx.

Nietzsche puts it all down to the will-to-power, says that the will-to-knowledge is a form of the will-to-power, and makes men of knowledge out to be the new heroes, knowing full well that, so far, bookish people have had least claim to glory of all socially significant people.

Start by giving over to the opposition: everything that's important is power, and this is asymmetrical with my knowledge and powerlessness being important. Then, illegitimate step: knowledge is important, knowledge is a form of power, and we're at the extremes where top and bottom switch, all the more so because you don't think so. Then: everything important is power and knowledge, knowledge has formerly been at the bottom of importance, but now that we're at the extremes knowledge and its accoutrements are all that's fundamentally important. And this is asymmetrical with power's deciding what's important for knowledge.

Before, power excluded knowledge by being inside it. Now, knowledge excludes power by being inside it. But when names are switched around, it's hard to remember what used to go where, which is what oriented one in the first place. Nietzsche got confused precisely because he found his answer, at which point the taken for granted became least obvious. I want to be important. For the first time in history my talents *are* important. I *am* important. But, above all, do not mistake me for someone else; I am dynamite because I know exactly how strong I like my tea, and why. That's never happened before. Is the only way I can be recognised the way of making myself spectacular, despite the fact that the spectacular belongs to the unspectacular now, and that what makes me spectacular is precisely that what I have to teach is how to recognise the spectacular in the unspectacular, in the so far unspectacular? Can't people see how spectacular the nooks and crannies are? Do I really need to teach them *everything* about it — am I really *that* important? Alright, I'll be god — my egoism isn't great enough not to try this.

The will-to-power: we do not know ourselves, we men of knowledge; we need to turn our will-to-truth, our form of the will-to-power, back on itself. For no other reason than that we *can*, for the first time, and that when we do, we find that the act of acquiring knowledge about oneself as completely as we can, involves all the excellences. It's the act of self-overcoming. That's our claim to fame: a self-propelling wheel. We, as individuals, can do what the entire society or species has done over millenia, in our own lifetimes. Instead of seeing the soul by examining the state, as Plato does, we can see the state by examining the soul.

Now we don't need anything from anyone else, except recognition. We are complete unto ourselves. We like being alone. But we like being alone partly because other people won't take responsibility for themselves, they impose on us with their taken-for-granted knowledge, so that we have to waste energy and right action in exchange for precious little real company. Recognition requires that the other person take a leap, a risk over the gap of our taken for granted knowledge, that s/he unmourn, invest something in us, to find us on the inside. The one thing we don't have, which has always been taken for granted, is recognition. We have all the things that haven't been taken for granted. I can be recognised for cultural flamboyance, daring, wit. Won't you recognise me for what *I* recognise in myself, my capacity to cope with hell which could have been avoided in a more encouraging and honest world as well as with, simultaneously, hell which is unavoidable for my kind of person, my capacity to be great and unknown, my ordinariness, the prissiness of my tea? *As well as* recognising me from the outside, as ultimately as insignificant or significant as anyone else, except, perhaps, to you?

It *is* possible, but Nietzsche never lived to find that out, because he didn't have anyone to talk to for long enough. The soul is a matter of the changes undergone by the body, and one has as complex a soul as one has time to have, and as complex a recognition as there is time to get. The one who is most in need of recognition takes the longest time to be in a position to get it. Because it takes the longest time to make the most complex simple enough to be what it is without cancelling itself out, at the extremes. And it involves going through the extremes, where it cancels itself out, to make it simple, to get away from the extremes to a new simplicity, which can be taken for granted and simply be what it is.

Forget the tea, forget the destiny, just look and listen. But first you have to know it's just tea, and you have to know it's destiny, before you can know how to appreciate that it's not just tea, and that it doesn't matter that it's destiny. If you know already, then you've missed Nietzsche. Because Nietzsche is very complicated, and his soul involves both of those steps and in that order. And once you can recognize him, then he's free to go forwards with you. Nietzsche never found out what it was like to go forwards in his own terms, or, rather, how to express that in his own terms, because there was no one who would take that leap to the inside, as well as leaping back to the outside, so that they would be someone different to Nietzsche who nevertheless recognised Nietzsche, so that he could talk to them, as someone different, and talk to them forwards, as recognising Nietzsche.

The magnificent is to be seen in the slime, in the one who overcomes him or herself, and doesn't overcome others, except inside her or himself. The unspectacular, the one who succeeds most when s/he appears most unsuccessful, the one who is invisible when s/he most deserves recognition of her/his excellence, Socrates' just man, this is the valuable one. To appreciate this one, one must appreciate the extent to which one does not appreciate him/her. One must risk the impossible, find the magnificent in the indifferent, the power in that which doesn't go anywhere. Perhaps it won't be there. But perhaps it will. Aristotle says that philosophy begins with wonder.

Nietzsche says that one's own world, one's own garden, begins with philosophy. Nietzsche begins with Aristotle. To appreciate Nietzsche, you have to appreciate Aristotle, and Nietzsche forgot that. To appreciate Nietzsche, you have to forget that too. But first you must appreciate it, otherwise, you've missed Nietzsche.

The good/evil epoch, which is founded in philosophy by Aristotle, is not an illness in the sense in which pregnancy is an illness. It is an illness *qua* illness, without qualification. It involves the demise of values, in which competition and the striving to overreach others becomes degraded into a competition of mediocrity and brutality, such as characterises the average male bar, and the average business climate, and the average political enterprise. And this is where we are, and what we have to work with.

The only way to change direction, at the extremes, is to keep going in the same direction. But this statement comes from a body of knowledge which does not take the extremes, the crisis of values, for granted, and is addressed to a body of knowledge which does. So in order to change direction we have to change our position in knowledge, and then keep going in the direction we were already travelling in.

The originally bad and contemptible, who have become the good, these are the ones in whom the future of value lies. The originally good, who became the evil, are of no significance whatsoever: evil is the old dead end of good, backwards. It is a relic, asymmetrical with the new dead end which can provide a taken for granted. Evil, and the original good, presuppose a community for which the individual is important, a community in which god and dead ancestors have a part. This is no longer the case. God is dead, the generation gap is a perpetually recurring fact of life, and the individual matters only to her/himself and to those who accidentally like her/him.

The only knowledge which is binding for more than one person is the knowledge that no knowledge is binding for more than one person, except by accident. And this is the knowledge of the originally bad, who belong to no family, no caste, no race, no good name, who are strangers in their own community. When, in the *Genealogy of Morals*, Nietzsche speaks of the lawless beast of prey which the evaluating person originally was, he must have known that he was speaking about the originally bad, that he was already revaluing that contemptible one, placing in her/him the values of the originally good. Because the hallmark of the contemptible was, in the noble/bad epoch, failure to belong, and to have a communal history. Not to be already recognised by the ancestors, and bear their name.

The point is that one wants to be recognised *as* one who isn't recognised, one wants to have respected the fact that one is not respected, and that part of one's experience and knowledge deals with that fact. This is the new dead end, the new taken for granted. And once one has a firm grip on this dead end, then one has recognised what one is and what one wants, one has power over one's own reality, and one ceases immediately to be at the extremes, and has firm power over the oscillations engendered by the opposing dead end in one's territory. One finds the other's oscillations in the context of one's own dead end instead of one's own dead end in the context of the other's oscillations. Then one can have a conversation in the context of which power struggles occur, instead of vice-versa. This is the meaning of Marx and Freud, one on the social level, the other on the individual.

What one wants is for the other person to recognise one as one who isn't recognised, before they recognise one simply. Because where one is, to be recognised, is not recognised; and after that has been recognised *as* that for long enough, one *is* recognised, and so can be recognised simply. For someone to recognise one as not recognised, without releasing that tension, just listening and registering and responding entirely in accordance with their condition so as not to disturb the paradox of yours, and to do so for long enough, requires that they are able to bend their knowledge, their attitudes, their power over reality, back on themselves: that is, that they are able to attempt honestly to recognise themselves. This is the Christian gift. But it also requires that they be able to do that without overflowing their bow-bent

94

tension on to you, which Christianity always did — hence the commanded proselytisation, the *responsibility* to proselytise. This latter capacity, to maintain the tension as a form of experience in its own right, as a tension which may never know release as a part of its workings or a part of its purpose, in certain contexts, this capacity is the noble correction to the Christian contribution. Together they complete the work of placing the operation of truth and knowledge within the context of taste, and the operation of personal power within the context of tastefully subtle knowledge, trained into the instincts.

And the only ones who can perform such a perverse combination, such a monstrous prodigy of aborted taste, are the bad and the evil. The truly evil can't survive that. Only the bad, who value life over principle, can. Never put passion before principle, *Karate Kid II* is told. But never put principle before life. That's just stupid, and all we have to value is intelligent sophistication. Recognition is all we can give each other, and people who can recognise are too rare and too valuable, too much to be appreciated, to treat them unjustly. These are the only ones with whom conversation, and genuine, non-Christian love is possible. To sacrifice the exception for the rule is sheer contemptible stupidity, and bad strategy to boot.

The third sideways journey is the same in content as the second, and the same in salient positions as the first, but radically different in content from the second because it's structured by the fact that the second sideways journey, its own reverse, happened before it. An experience of pertinent nonsense shakes the taken-for-granted sense of knowledge, and allows a just appreciation of alternative knowledge. The noble has been tamed with respect to society; but now, for the first time, s/he is free to be untamed with respect to him/herself, to overcome her/his values in whichever direction s/he may choose. And society no longer means a thing.

The bad, who were bad because society never did mean anything to them, are free for the first time to pursue their interests at least to the degree anyone else is. To be wrong, without their entire reality being discounted every time they make a mistake. But the noble and the bad, which is the same as the noble and the Christian good, can only coincide after they've been ripped apart, after the mourning, which occurs on either side of the second movement.

Freud has taught us this: how to create a beginning which never happened, the Oedipal complex, a mourning for a penis which was never lost, by repeating it a second time in the analysis of what one knows without knowing it, what one takes for granted by repeating it instead of remembering it. There's a male way to do it, and a female way to do it, and they are upside down in relation to each other and not symmetrical with respect to each other.

And then one can completely have a part, instead of simply being apart. One can leave one's penis at the door, because no one who knows what they're doing really cares enough to take it away. There's nothing at stake. God, the primal and castrating father, is dead. And, with him, the unassailable nature of the taboo against touching, which is what permits the formation of classes of untouchables. It doesn't matter what you do, only that you're good at it — excellence, *arete.* And that statement comes from a body of knowledge which takes it for granted that intelligence is necessary and good if one is to have anything other than imagined integrity, and that real integrity is essential if one is to follow through one's intelligence to the point of knowledge about knowledge.

At that point you can concede that the other knows something, but that nothing, at bottom, is at stake. The other knows something, has some power over reality, but, at bottom, that's nothing. I know something too; and, at bottom, there's nothing at stake; that's nothing. This is the meaning of Lacan. Then we can make our own knowledges by looping out sideways around each other's taken for granteds. This is the way knowledge has always worked, at bottom, but now there is perverted knowledge as well as straight knowledge. Straight knowledge is, at bottom, perverted. And perverted knowledge is, at bottom, straight. The only way to be really straight is to be prepared to be really perverted. And vice-versa.

The pervert, however, is in a position to be straight or perverted. The straight person can only be perverted. Really good people can oly be found in the wrong places.

Nietzsche failed to distinguish between the extremes and where the extremes are taken for granted. The eternal return applies only at the extremes. Move away from the extremes, and it's irrelevant. The death of god applies only at the extremes; away, it's irrelevant. On the before side of the extremes, it's really bad, because life is health, and the disease part of it has eaten it away. On the after side of the extremes, it's quite good, because life is disease, and there's a choice about the health part of it. The eternal return becomes the repetition compulsion, inside one, which powers creativity under the impulsion of the death which includes life, instead of vice-versa.

When I wake, all I see is death; when I sleep, dreams. Thus Heraclitus. Nothing's changed. But then it was bad, and now it's good. At the extremes, there is no bad or good, and everything changes and nothing changes. Having passed through the extremes twice, backwards and forwards, in the time of Heraclitus and Parmenides and in the time of Marx and Nietzsche, we're now able to choose which side of the extremes we want to be on. And the fact that we can choose allows us to be on both sides.

What I like about Socrates, especially, is what he didn't say. I am wise and a destiny. I repudiate my ancestry. I like tea. Please take care, above all, not to mistake me for anyone else, particularly not Wagner. I despise the improvers of mankind. I'm having the anti-Semites shot and I'm saving the world. If you prick me, do I not bleed?

Why does it matter, Nietzsche? Only because you know it doesn't, sugar.

Justice, according to Plato, is a matter of putting everything in its own place. At the extremes, we're in a position to see that that requires taking the place of order itself into consideration, and that immediately puts the right places in the wrong places, until one is away from the extremes. One has to see the thing from the inside and from the outside to do justice to it from its own point of view as well as doing other pieces their own justice. That means going backwards and forwards, bending oneself backwards on oneself, bending each of the pieces back on themselves, so that they can recognise themselves as they are from the inside, forwards, and recognise each other as the other is from the inside, by contrast with each other. Then they can choose, assert, their own places intelligently, according to their own wants.

The first step is to recognise that they want to be recognised as not being recognised, because that is where they are and therefore the only place in which they can be accurately recognised. They want to be included as excluded, so that with two more steps they can be excluded as included, like anybody else.

Marx noted the importance of this ordering in the Preface to *Capital* in which he pointed out, like Aristotle, that the order of exposition of knowledge is the reverse of the order of inquiry. What he failed to note is that, at the extremes, the place of order itself is in question, so that order itself has to undergo a back-and-forth movement, knowing what it's doing in the order of exposition, and not knowing what it's doing in the order of inquiry, so that the inquiry can form a part of the exposition, and the exposition can form a part of the inquiry. Away from the extremes, exposition is exposition and inquiry is inquiry. At the extremes they have to swing through one another repeatedly, so that order itself is not taken for granted.

But they have to swing through one another in the right wrong order to give all parties their due. That means that they must swing through one another in such a way as to bend back on themselves, so that they can find their taken for granted in themselves and not require the other to give it to them: they must swing through each other in such a way as to leave the other with what the other wants. Only after that can there be justice, when each party knows what it wants. The inquiry knows that it wants to lack an answer, and the exposition knows that it wants to lack a question. The one wants the other to take up where it leaves off. What they want to do is what they were doing already, which is to swing through one another. But now, when they're going forwards, having been bent back on themselves to recognise themselves in the right order, they can do that justly, and the order doesn't really matter any more, because they can each find what they want elsewhere now that they know what they want.

[A note to the reader: if the preceding paragraph is read so that "what one wants" means "what one is wanting in" or "what one lacks," then the way meanings work at the extremes will be evident. If both meanings are kept in mind, the interaction between the extremes and away from the extremes will be evident. Read the extreme way, "finding what one wants elsewhere" can mean finding it where one originally was, where it (what one wants) has the non-extreme meaning, more than the meaning of what one lacks.]

The right order, here, is first, to recognise oneself as: wanting to be recognised as not being recognised; and then to recognise oneself as being recognised in that act; and then to recognise oneself as whatever one is in one's own eyes; and then to do or get what one wants. Of course, this is the wrong order, because it starts at the end. But it's the right wrong order, because it gets you where you want to go without having to defend yourself in advance. It's the way knowledge has always worked. There's no right place to start, at bottom, only wrong ones. This is the meaning of Heidegger.

In our society, we've reached the bottom, we can pick our wrong places to start. And, since we're included in knowledge, if we take ourselves seriously, we take knowledge seriously. And then the issue of justice becomes very important, because knowledge is a form of power, if you take it seriously enough not to take it for granted, and then you find you're being oppressed by other people's taken for granted knowledge, particularly because you take knowledge seriously. That's when you learn respect for just dealings, and, with it, respect for those who are usually taken for granted as bad or indifferent. And contempt for those who are usually taken for granted as respectworthy.

Life is a disease. If you work that out, all you can do to communicate is to go backwards, or sideways. If you communicate forwards you land up talking in the terms of the knowledge for which life is health. At that point communication itself is a piece of the disease destroying your piece of the disease. Then, to get back where you want to be you still have to go backwards, or sideways, in the right wrong order, starting implicitly or explicitly at the end. The only way to communicate with a body of taken-for-granted knowledge, from the outside, is to start off by not communicating.

Unless there are two of you who are disease people. Then you can both talk without imposing your realities on each other, simply appreciating, rejecting, or enjoying each other, and all that I've written here is irrelevant except as a kind of fine tuning, or as background music for when things have gone wrong, or as a performance or display. In that case it's really a dissertation on rhetoric and strategy.

Knowledge is a form of power. When one has removed oneself from the taken for granted, the most obvious thing becomes the most surprising, the hardest to find. What you want becomes very hard to find, to identify. What to do with knowledge becomes very hard to find. What to do with personal power becomes very hard to find. The answer is in the old taken-for-granted knowledge. The answer is what one was already aiming to do with these things, that is what one wants. You don't get to that point of difficulty and loss unless you wanted something very badly.

Now you've found a way of saying what you could only tend towards before; but you were only tending towards it on the basis of that taken-for-granted reality. Now you can say it and live it, but you're no longer in the only place it made sense to look for it and have it. The order of inquiry lacks an answer, and the order of exposition, which comes once one has completed one's inquiry, lacks a question. So you recognise yourself as not being recognised by yourself. And so on: you've made yourself a real starting point for your own power over reality. You can be just to yourself, because you're outside knowledge. And you can mourn back in as you mourned out, switching what you want to switch, committing yourself, and commiting yourself thoroughly, deliberately and completely to new or the same priorities and values. Forwards, backwards, forwards. And you can concede that you knew something before, but nothing's at stake, so that's nothing. You know something now. But nothing's at stake. So that's nothing.

Nietzsche, Freud, and Marx all wanted something from society. Now there's no society to give anything human that counts, only individuals. Knowledge and power are for defending yourself against other people's taken-for-granted knowledge, and for overcoming yourself in directions of your choice. Anything other than that is stupid, crass, and contemptible. That's the way things are. Of course, you're perfectly free to be stupid, crass, and contemptible. But that doesn't alter the facts.

If you do it right, *you'll* usually look contemptible, and you'll usually look as though *you're* being gratuitously aggressive and hostile. And, from the other point of view, you will be. And that's also the way things are. But if you know where you stand, in a way you can relax into, you can explain how two different taken for granteds can swing through one another sideways so that they come out with integrity and talking to one another for the first time. No change in knowledge. Just a change in you. And that explanation already takes you sideways: the other person takes the offer, or s/he doesn't. Just, both ways.

This is why knowledge about knowledge is the one thing that cannot be brought back to life. The only intelligent — fully conscious, knowing — use of knowledge is to overcome knowledge. Who wants to know? Life is a disease, and, at bottom, it's horrible. Art, which is the best we can do, is the biggest lie. Its truth lies in its fulfilment of the human yearning to deceive itself about life. To make people know is strictly an aggressive act, and, if you place any value on human experience at all, you should do so only in self-defence or when at the extremes.

Knowledge is a form of power. The subjects of knowledge who take it for granted, and therefore do not know that it is a form of power, have their reality constituted for them in advance; their power over reality is taken out of their control; they are castrated. Those who know that knowledge is a form of power no longer take it for granted. It therefore no longer has power over reality for them. They have abandoned their power over reality; they have castrated the power of knowledge itself; they themselves are effectively castrated.

From their point of view, however, the subjects of taken-for-granted knowledge are exercising power without control and without restraint, without knowing what they are doing. The former are powerless because they know that they know, they are able to exercise restraint, maintain the tension, because they are not controlled by knowledge. The latter are powerful because they do not know that they know, they are unable to exercise restraint because they are entirely controlled by knowledge. This is at the extremes, where the taken for granted becomes what catches you by surprise.

What we have is Nietzsche's fable of the eagles and sheep, given its final twist the perverted way, the eagle whose greatness lies in the manner in which s/he is able to restrain him/herself, not because s/he is lacking in voraciousness and ferocity, but precisely because s/he isn't. Why not?

In fact, this twist is crucial to Nietzsche; it is everything towards which his work strives. As he says, great love, which is truly love, depends on great self-love. And he also says the reverse.

To continue: you start off wanting to get away from the oppression of other people's taken-for-granted knowledge and get power over yourself, self-knowledge, so that you can live with integrity. And you find that the process of getting power over yourself loses you both power over those who oppress you and power over yourself. And that's not symmetrical with power over yourself, including the power to deal with other people. They don't know they're castrated, so, effectively, they aren't. You know you're castrated, so, effectively, you are. You know what it means to know, so you know nothing immediately powerful or effective: knowledge is no longer a form of power, precisely because you've come to know it is. They don't know what it means to know, so everything they know is powerful. You're perfectly contemptible, now, and perfectly incapable of defending yourself, of effectively registering your values on the world. You've lost to the opposition, given yourself over entirely, precisely by trying the only way to overcome it. Like Faust, you've exchanged your soul for the knowledge that mattered only to your soul.

That's at the extremes, where you know that life is hell because that's the way things are. But you know that if they knew what they knew, if they had self-knowledge, they would know that they knew nothing, too. Which means that

103

your ignorance and your consequent powerlessness, your castration, includes their knowledge, their power over reality, their penis. And so you loop yourself sideways around their taken for granted knowledge. You start by recognising yourself as: wanting to be recognised as someone who isn't recognised, knowing yourself as someone who doesn't know, being conscious of yourself as someone who isn't conscious. And then you're at your own dead end, and ready to reclaim your aim, which you left behind in the territory of taken for granted knowledge. How to hide something where you can't find it, so that it can't be stolen from you: blatantly placed in the most obvious of places, and in the opposition's territory.

And you get your aim back by looping yourself sideways around their taken for granteds, which still project into your territory, because your territory now includes theirs. And you consolidate that by repeating it, repeating the sideways loops, again and again. Because all you need other people for is their recognition, their company for you where you are, which is someone who knows that s/he doesn't know, and whose ignorance includes their taken-for-granted knowledge. The only place for knowledge is the castration of knowledge; the only place for knowledge for more than one person is the knowledge that there is no knowledge in a place for more than one person, except by the accident of who the other person happens to be.

If you don't want company which will be company for you where you are, wanting to relax into something taken for granted like anybody else, then it doesn't matter. Become a politician. If you want the recognition that company entails, then all that matters is the looping sideways, back and forth. If the other person leaps, and leaps back, successively and simultaneously, then you have company, recognising you because they leaped, different to you because they leaped back. If they don't leap, you get hurt, but it was *your* aim, then, to have real company, and not also theirs, and the outcome is just. Then you mourn on your own, and you can regard them as stupid, because it really doesn't matter to anyone but you. God is dead. And if it does matter to them, then they will also be mourning, even if they don't know it.

Knowledge is the one thing that can't be brought back to life, because knowledge is now the one thing we know about, and the only thing we fully know about. We know what we know, and we know what we don't want to know, what we want to take for granted, and what we don't want to take for granted. And that's all that we know. We know what knowledge is, and we know what knowledge does; the only further concern we can have with knowledge is what we want to do with it, how we want to use it. We can be just, or we can be unjust; that's the only choice we have in regard to knowledge. There are many ways to be unjust, and they're all dominated by a single knowledge, a single highest good. There is only one way to be just, and it follows the many paths between many knowledges. To tread that path, one has to have started by recognising one's submission to the one knowledge — which will not be a submission, something that one can change, until one has made it so by recognising it in that way — and then one has to have bent that knowledge back on itself. After that, recognition comes only from those others who have done the same. For the rest, justice occurs only in the realm of the invisible, or in the visible if they are too naive to know better. The latter are valued by those who don't know; the former are especially valued by those who know with excellence; the avant-garde of knowledge value nothing.

According to Freud, the will-to-knowledge is an ethical transformation of the sadistic drive, the will-to-power, which finds its source in the anal zone. Between the oral phase, in which one's desire does not yet have whole objects to relate to in a simple way, and the phallic phase, in which one abandons and mourns one's penis, so that one can subordinate one's will-to-power to a search for one's penis elsewhere. In analysis, one runs it according to the ego's resistances and defences, so it goes backwards, starting in the middle with anal knowledge, and dealing in that context with desire for one's penis and for bits and pieces of the delicious. In the end, if you want company, you have to accept that your penis never went away, or that you never had it, and that you can only have delicious bits and pieces if you're prepared to pay close attention to your anal zone.

If you don't want company, it doesn't matter if you don't respect your own products, and remain purely a consumer of the products of others. That is, a consumer whose production is included by consumption, instead of the other way round.

Knowledge is a form of power, and has castrated everything, including, at the extremes, at bottom, itself. This means that we are free to jump the gap and castrate our own castration, double and quits. Then we're worse off but we're a lot more excellent. That's what having balls means. In the thought that stretches from Heraclitus and Parmenides to Hegel, this reads: having balls means having a vagina if you haven't, and having a penis if you have a vagina. This means: being prepared to fall on your ass, because nothing's at stake, but falling on your ass well, because you want there to be something at stake.

What does a woman want? A woman wants to be allowed to have an asshole without having to defend herself in advance, so that she has some space, some room to manoeuvre, to decide what she wants to do with her vagina. The feminist movement forgot, and got lost in the asshole. A man wants to keep the asshole to himself, so that no one else can get in and so that he can disappear into it when his dick's in trouble. He's already decided what to do with his dick: he wants to keep it untouched as a display piece. Apparently if another man plays with it then it's not fulfilling its function in an important way. Clearly, then, what's at stake is that another asshole might take it away, or make one want to give it away. Which is true, and sensibly prudent, since men are all the same. A woman, on the other hand, doesn't have an asshole which she can decide what to do with, so there's no temptation for a man to lose it there. Now women are discovering their assholes, so men have to take responsibility for their power. And that's hell, which is why they turned it into knowledge in the first place.

But now that knowledge is being turned into power, and men have to crawl out of their anal zones, they forget, and get lost in the unprotected air of honesty and satisfying company. It's hell out there. Time to manage the asshole again, not the asshole in the sense in which the vagina is an asshole, but an asshole *qua* asshole, without qualification, for which the only way out is the way in, repeatedly, until not getting anywhere, backwards and forwards, becomes very delicious, at which point you can get off. And you can decide what to do with your penis, or if you want to do anything with it, yourself, at all. Courage, justice, forbearance, knowledge about knowledge. Just look where they've all gone!

Plato and Nietzsche were great artists, and therefore diarrhoeac. The rest were constipated. Wittgenstein, waiting at the dead end, was the only true philosopher, and he was very depressed.

At bottom, the question is, who gives a shit?

Tea, anyone?

Prologue and Poem

Theseus: "Where are you?"
Minotaur: "I'm hiding!"
Theseus: "Where are you? I bought those gold earings
        you wanted."
Minotaur: "I'm hiding — in the front cloooset!"

You know, the Muses still do speak
They spread the wine as thickly on the glazed
Banquet of a fructifying summer sheen
On pools of moss encrusted foliage reflected
Wavering in surfaces of foliage in the shade

It's true. The Muses still do speak
But not the fair proportioned dainty
Ones, the comfortable picnic undisturbed
And swathed in artful drapes serenely
Festival observer unobserved and all but there

Oh no — the Muses still do speak
But now they whisper Sybilline clarion
And call in winding echoes through a more
Reverberating and in tumult more increasing
More in hidden in more lost less whispering places

Eulogy: How to Speak Well

Oh yes — the Muses still do speak
More violently they carve the hurtling
Shadow of a mighty lost Elysian less losing
Grow and shine forth fleeting in the May fly
Long ago the labyrinth now we are and when

It's true. The Muses still do speak
But now they cry the thin elusive clarion
Of a floating broad not here and staggering
Where   the blow   it passes sinuous and uncoils
Flatly in its slender grow and cover under whole

Why not? The Muses still do speak
And crying gently in the music play
The leaves they rustle but no more of that
The global vestige leaves   no loss and flies
To flatten swell and how   where are we   there

Part Two

In Freud's Defence : ecnefeD s'duerF nI
In Freud's Defence

Introduction to Part Two

The following very important fact is almost universally overlooked: a theory is just a theory. It is true that our familiar perceptions and spontaneous ideas also are parts of a kind of a theory which we generally take for granted. They come about, it is true, partly under the influence of explicit theories; they are packed with prejudices and assumptions which have no bearing on reality; they can be argued, proved, disproved, changed; they have a history, even if its movement — as is often the case — is too slow to have to be taken seriously in an individual lifetime. But a rigorously and carefully worked out theory is a theory in a different way. It takes a different kind of effort, a special effort, to make it familiar and taken for granted, to forget that it has a history and is not one with Nature. A theory is therefore *all the more* just a theory *the more* it is carefully and rigorously worked out.

Just *because* a theory is carefully and rigorously worked out, it perpetually reminds itself, in almost every sentence of its presentation, that it is not the same as our familiar views. If it *were* the same, it wouldn't *have* to be carefully worked out and presented, since we would all know it and be familiar with it anyway. There'd be no point in it. It reminds itself perpetually, then, that it is not the same as our familiar views, or as other theories: it reminds itself perpetually that it is just a theory.

It therefore opens a passage, in almost every sentence of its presentation, to the alternatives presented by other theories and by our familiar views. It also *relies* on them, to communicate and present itself, and to convince us of its validity and truth for us. And the *more*, therefore, that it tries to change our views about *everything* in its chosen field, the *more* it affirms and relies on these other views as they are when *completely* unchanged by it.

It is, after all, just a theory. If it tries to change our views about *everything* in a field it has chosen, it throws into as clear a contrast as possible what our views are as opposed to its new view. It tries to change what is the meaning for us of *everything* in its chosen field; if it succeeds, it succeeds also in highlighting for us what the meanings of those everythings, which it is trying to change, already are for us.

To the extent that it succeeds in making itself meaningful, to that extent it succeeds in making the views meaningful which it tries to change. To the extent that is succeeds in being carefully worked out and rigorous, it reminds itself, to that extent, in almost every one of its sentences, of the meaningfulness of the views from which it succeeds in departing and which it succeeds in changing.

It relies on these other views, it opens up passages to them, and it demonstrates their meaning, validity and truth for us in almost every one of its sentences, in the degree that it succeeds in presenting itself as a meaningful, reliable and valid view of its chosen field.

It is a theory, and it is a theory developed for a particular kind of purpose or kinds of purposes. It has no bearing on the other views it tries to change when they are held outside of those purposes, because its own meaning is strictly limited to the field established by those purposes. And the more it succeeds, *within* the limits of its purposes (stated or not), the more it positively *supports* and encourages, within those limits, the views to which it succeeds in presenting an alternative.

When Freud, for example, says everything in the field of psychology is a form of sexuality and aggression, he is changing, often subtly, what we mean by sexuality and aggression, and he is changing, often subtly, what we mean by all the other things he is now calling forms of sexuality and aggression. Something by a new name still is and does all the things it was and did under the old name: we just notice and engage with different things about it. A theory is just a theory: noticing the different and new things about its field of relevance doesn't make the old things we noticed about that field go away. In fact, it throws them into strong relief and brings their meaning for us out more strongly as they already are the more it succeeds in making them different for us from what they already are.

A theory is just a theory. When it becomes familiar and taken for granted, then it isn't just a theory any more. But then there are or will be new theories. And they are or will be just theories. For us, at the time, then, a theory is just a theory, requiring a special kind of effort to make it familiar and taken for granted, to forget that it has a history and isn't just one with Nature. For us, at the time, then, a theory should be treated as such.

The following is an attempt to treat Freud's theory as such, as just a theory, relying on, opening up passages to, and bringing out or demonstrating the meaning, validity and truth for us of every view and position it opposes and attempts to change.

In Freud's Defence : ecnefeD s'duerF nI
In Freud's Defence

The part of this study which follows cannot be given to the public without extensive explanations and apologies... I found myself unable to wipe out the traces of the history of the work's origin, which was in any case unusual.

Actually it has been written twice: for the first time a few years ago in Vienna, where I did not think it would be possible to publish it. I determined to give it up; but it tormented me like an unlaid ghost, and I found a way out by making two pieces of it independent and publishing them in our periodical *Imago*... The remainder... I held back, as I thought, forever... I had scarcely arrived in England before I found the temptation irresistible to make the knowledge I had held back accessible to the world, and I began to revise the third part of my study to fit it on to the two parts that had already been published. This naturally involved a partial rearrangement of the material. I did not succeed, however, in including the whole of this material in my second version; on the other hand I could not make up my mind to give up the earlier versions entirely. And so it has come about that I have adopted the expedient of attaching a whole piece of the first presentation to the second unchanged — which has brought with it the disadvantage of involving extensive repetition.

...it can be no misfortune if the public is obliged to read the same thing... twice over. There are things which should be said more than once and which cannot be said often enough. But the reader must decide of his own free will whether to linger over the subject or to come back to it. He must not be surreptitiously led into having the same thing put before him twice in one book. It is a piece of clumsiness for which the author must take the blame. Unluckily an author's creative power does not always obey his will: the work proceeds as it can, and often presents itself to the author as something independent or even alien.

Freud[1]

...the consequences of what Freud says about *Verneinung* as a form of avowal — to say the least, it cannot be treated as the equivalent of just any old thing.

This is how theory describes the way in which resistance is engendered in practice. It is also what I mean when I say that there is no other resistance to analysis than that of the analyst himself.

...The serious thing is that with present-day authors the sequence of analytic effects seems to be understood inside out.

Lacan[2]

There was a young lady from Niger
Who smiled as she rode on a tiger
They came back from the ride
With the lady inside
And the smile on the face of the tiger

Anon.

Freud defends his cosmological writings as speculation, not to be given the same seriousness of critical attention as his non-speculative work. "But what is already hidden from him is the connection — which is always demonstrable — between the occasion on which this expectant anxiety arises and the danger which it conjures up. Thus a ceremonial starts as an *action for defence* or *insurance, a protective measure.*"[3]

Denial, as he tells us, does not necessarily mean that something is not the case, but may well mean rather that this something is the case in another knowledge, another set of reference points, with which the knowledge of the denier wants nothing to do. It is possible, then, that Freud's speculation holds the most serious key to his non-speculative work, and that, conversely, the points of reference offered by his non-speculative work may provide us with the means of understanding his defence of his speculation as to be less critically attended to.

As in any analysis, it is necessary to begin with his resistances and trace their path backwards, undoing them as we go, so that the forward direction may be followed of the new resistances that are presupposed in order to realise and articulate Freud's motivating phantasy.[4] For, of course, all consciousness presupposes resistances to what is unconscious, before analysis and also after it. I shall attempt to trace the skeleton of such an analysis. And "if in the end that hypothesis bears a highly improbable appearance, that need be no argument against the possibility of its approximating more or less closely to the reality which it is so hard to reconstruct."[5]

Freud had a particular purpose in mind when he constucted his theories of human motivation, a purpose which, if he was astute, precisely directed the angle at which his views on life and death approached the more purely therapeutic body of his work. We need ascribe no purposes to nature or the cosmos, and no knowledge can claim to be securely grounded which depends on the postulation of such purposes. But insofar as the thinking human being has purposes, and aims to change her/his condition via the mediation of her/his thought, no knowledge can claim to be true to its reality which does not postulate a purpose that it is intended to serve; nor can it claim, in this default, to be more than idle entertainment. Knowledge which is relevant to the active human being is therefore never securely grounded when it comes to its pertinence to nature or to the cosmos in the sense in which they are independent of human concerns. But knowledge only exists, as more than idle entertainment, for the purposes of the active human being, so that there is no knowledge worthy of the name for which there is a nature or cosmos independent of purposes, specifically human purposes, in the context of which alone the knowledge is found which in turn provides the context for what we understand by nature or cosmos. "The problem of the nature of the world without regard to our percipient mental apparatus is an empty abstraction, devoid of practical interest."[6]

Knowledge which ascribes purposes to nature is therefore perfectly well grounded, as long as it knows that knowledge outside of human purposes is an illusion, that the god who founds such knowledge is dead, and that the distinction to be made is not between knowledge of human concerns and knowledge of nature, but between knowledge that does as it pleases well and knowledge that does as it pleases badly, each of the latter pair including both of the former pair.

The fear of castration, according to Freud, who was good at knowledge, boils down to a fear of being overwhelmed by too much stimulation from within, which is equivalent to fearing the absence of the saving object from without.

> The high degree of narcissistic value which the penis possesses can appeal to the fact that the organ is a guarantee to its owner that he can be once more united to his mother — i.e. to a substitute for her — in the act of copulation. Being deprived of it amounts to a renewed separatlon from her, and this in its turn means being helplessly exposed to an unpleasurable tension due to instinctual need, as was the case at birth...
>
> The progress which the child makes in its

development — its growing independence, the sharper division of its mental apparatus into several agencies, the advent of new needs — cannot fail to exert an influence upon the content of the danger-situation. We have already traced the change of that content from loss of the mother as an object to castration.[7]

It boils down, that is, to the unpleasure principle, the psychic registering of the principle of constancy, the violation of which disrupts the organism's tolerable constellation of forces.

We may infer, therefore, that the fear of castration is only one possible form in which the organism's relation to its own constellation of forces represents itself to the organism, and that this relation can conceivably be grasped and responded to via the mediation of very different forms of representation. And, indeed, Freud tells us that, in the case of women, the fear of overwhelming stimulation is grasped in the form of fear of loss of love, since the penis is already absent and is not therefore an object which can be further absent without more ado.[8] Later, of course, there is more ado, which, although it amounts to much ado about nothing, is nonetheless full of sound and fury.

If we are to dispense with divine providence and the existence of human aims outside of human beings, we have no recourse but to attribute the development of the human organism to the material conditions of its history, and to assume that what we find ontogenetically we shall be able to see in the course of its earlier production, more gradual and writ large, in phylogenetic conditions and experience. It was good enough for Plato, it was good enough for Marx, and it's good enough for Freud. The individual and the species are internally related, from the point of view of any knowledge worthy of the name. That is, each is what it *is* only in relation to the other; what each *is* involves the other: they are *logically* related, not only related by the *fact* of the historical accident of being associated with each other.

The principle of constancy, registered psychologically as the unpleasure principle, can thus be taken to be a way of talking about the logic of the individual, the principle describing its being what it is, since this principle is what it all boils down to, and since this principle involves a fundamental relation to the mother, the first representative of society.

What we have here is a whole in which all the parts get their meaning from each other, since they have nothing else from which to get it. A whole entire unto itself, and consequently parts none of which is entire unto itself, since any statement about any part, if it says something about that part, can get that something only from some other part of the whole, the whole being all there is.

At the commencement of its individual existence, the human organism is helpless in the face of its internal stimulation, and is in fact distinguished by the prolongation and degree of this helplessness in relation to the newborn of any other species. At the end of its typical, its species-specific, development, at the point at which it becomes an adult individual capable of procuring its idiosyncratic love and its idiosyncratic work, the human organism is a highly differentiated constellation of forces the principle of whose operation is the constancy or unpleasure principle. In accordance with this principle powerful barriers are set up against intense internal stimulation, so that the organism's intensities are able to emerge only as deflected into highly organised channels which are made available to them by the same defensive barrier which deflects them.

Consequently all civilised activity is a compromise formation, a symptom compromising between unorganised quantitative intensity and qualitatively differentiated organisation. The civilised activities to which this applies include thinking and the acquisition or production of knowledge. "The whole flux of our mental life and everything that finds expression in our thoughts are derivations and representa-

122

tives of the multifarious instincts that are innate in our physical constitution."[9] And, "speeches are themselves symptoms and, like them arise from compromises between the conscious and the unconscious."[10]

What is responsible for this change, according to Freud, is the resolution of the Oedipal complex, as a consequence of fear of castration in males, and as a consequence of acceptance of castration in females, the latter — the acceptance of castration — taking the further form of representation, or finding its equivalent in, the desire for a baby attained through the love of a man.[11] The result of this resolution of the Oedipal complex is that the organism has turned its intensities against themselves, replacing its former undifferentiated character with a differentiation into the id, the locus of the unorganised and dangerous intensities; the ego, the locus of individual organisation which can help itself; and the superego, the locus of morality, of social organisation which provides not only for the needs of the individuals who are in a helpless condition, but also takes further arms against external dangers to the individual and society, and in addition proliferates its own specific contributions. "It is in keeping with the course of human development that external coercion gradually becomes internalised.... Such a strengthening of the superego is a most precious cultural asset in the psychological field. Those in whom it has taken place are turned from being opponents of civilisation into being its vehicles."[12]

The whole, none of the parts of which are entire unto themselves, is capable of producing parts which are sufficiently different as to have opposite meanings and effects. The parts depend on each other for their meaning in such a way as to have entirely independent meanings. The rigorous commitment to thinking in terms of a whole, without an external object, results in a whole divided against itself, external to itself.

The superego is a precipitate of identifications of the ego with the parents, as embodiments of authority, of help against the overwhelming, and of the power to castrate.[13] This power to castrate, as we have seen, is given its significance by the importance of the loss of an external object with power to save the helpless infant from overwhelming stimulation from within. The loss of the penis is the loss of a means to ensure or gain that help, and so comes to form an equivalent to that latter loss in the organism's representations of its relevant world, and, indeed, of what is most salient to it in its world.

Castration plays the role in the individual's development and character, which development and character is the subject matter or content of Freud's theory, that is played by the division-against-itself correlative with thinking a whole entire unto itself in the development and character of Freud's theory itself, which is the form and principle in terms of which the subject matter is understood.

We can infer, from the phylogenetic point of view, that, while it may have been necessary for the organism to develop in such a way that it was turned back on itself, in order to avert disintegration or helplessness in the face of overwhelming internal excitation, the specific form which its involution or invagination took, via the internalisation of the parental figures, could only have come about as a result of a concatenation of historical accidents, there being nothing outside the whole to guide the process of the whole's becomning what it is. The whole itself can only be explained in terms of its parts, there being nothing else, and in terms of accidental relations of parts, which do *not* yet depend on each other for their meaning, since the whole we find we have to explain does not yet exist while it is coming to be, so that the parts do not yet have to depend for their meaning on each other. They are not yet parts of the whole; their meaning, what they are, is not yet fixed as being parts of all there is. As Freud says in connection with mental processes:

So long as we trace the development from its

final outcome backwards, the chain of events appears continuous, and we feel we have gained an insight which is completely satisfactory or even exhaustive. But if we proceed the reverse way, if we start from the premises inferred from the analysis and try to follow these up to the final result, then we no longer get the impression of an inevitable sequence of events which could not have been otherwise determined. We notice at once that there might have been another result, and that we might have been just as well able to understand and explain the latter. The synthesis is thus not so satisfactory as the analysis; in other words, from a knowledge of the premises we could not have foretold the nature of the result.[14]

The rigorous commitment to thinking in terms of a whole, entire unto itself, is also a commitment to thinking outside the context of that whole, if the character of the whole itself is to be described and made meaningful, made sense of.

We can infer, too, that the more complex society became, so that it became an increasingly complex and all-encompassing part of the organism's relevant exterior, the more complex and all-encompassing the barriers against disorganised intensity within the organism had to become if it was not to be abandoned to its helpless condition when in isolation. This is evident from the relative degree of prevalent free-floating anxiety — the psychological signal that there is danger from internal sources — on which Freud remarks in primitive societies.[15]

The fear of death, of course, requires to be explained before it can serve as an explanatory factor. And Freud explains how death becomes salient to an organism which could not yet have experienced it, by means of the overwhelming by internal stimulation from which castration fear, too, takes its significance and saliency to the organism: each is a form of representation in which that overwhelming is grasped and responded to, or a registration which, as a compromise formation, is itself a response or a part of a response: "the unconscious seems to contain nothing that could give any content to our concept of the annihilation of life... I am therefore inclined to adhere to the view that the fear of death should be regarded as analogous to the fear of castration and that the situation to which the ego is reacting is one of being abandoned by the protecting super-ego — the powers of destiny — so that it has no longer any safeguard against all the dangers that surround it."[16] And

> The individual will have made an important advance in his capacity for self-preservation if he can foresee and expect a traumatic situation of this kind which entails helplessness, instead of simply waiting for it to happen. Let us call a situation which contains the determinant for such an expectation a danger-situation. It is in this situation that the signal of anxiety is given. The signal announces, "I am expecting a situation of helplessness to set in," or: "The present situation reminds me of one of the traumatic experiences I have had before. Therefore I will anticipate the trauma and behave as though it had already come, while there is yet time to turn it aside." Anxiety is therefore on the one hand an expectation of a trauma, and on the other a repetition of it in a mitigated form.[17]

Again, "this change constitutes a first great step forward in the provision made by the infant for its self-preservation, and at the same time represents a transition from the automatic and involuntary fresh appearance of anxiety to the intentional reproduction of anxiety as a signal of danger."[18]

An inscription in the organism's functioning, in the constellation of forces that constitute it, make it what it is, an inscription which is itself part of the act of inscribing, part of the bending backwards or inwards on itself of the developing organism.[19]

The relation of the individual to what is beyond the whole, or at the limits of the whole itself — death — must be accounted for in terms of what is inside the whole, the whole being all there is. The correlative relation in the *theory* which allows us to say this is given by the term "the unconscious," an outside of the theory which is inside it. *All* the ideas giving the details of the working of the unconscious must in the end divide against themselves and be external to themselves in accordance with the character of the idea of which they give the details. They do not therefore mean what they ordinarily mean: they rather give us clues to making sense of this other kind of meaning, this other kind of sense or logic, which holds two things together in one by keeping them apart as two.

Clearly, one of the crucial changes which occurs in the organism's development from a state of helpless disorganisation in the face of internal and external dangers to a state of organised, efficacious will to change external and internal circumstances, from a state of powerlessness in the face of undifferentiated reality to a state of individual power over internal and external reality, is a change from a state of experience for which time has no salience to a state of experience in which time plays a part that consists in making space for alternative paths to be established and followed: "A danger-situation is a recognized, remembered, expected situation of helplessness. Anxiety is the original reaction to helplessness in the trauma and is reproduced later on in the danger-situation as a signal for help. The ego, which experienced the trauma passively, now repeats it actively in a weakened version, in the hope of being able itself to direct its course."[20]

Freud draws explicit attention to the significance of the relevance or saliency of time as a differentiating characteristic in his analysis of the human organism:

> Restraint of motor discharge (of action) had now become necessary, and was provided by means of the process of *thought*, which was developed from ideation. Thought was endowed with qualities which made it possible for the mental apparatus to support increased tension during a delay in the process of discharge.[21]

Since his is an account not only of the structure and functioning of human beings at any given time, but also of the development and origin of that structure and functioning in the course of time, it is clear that what he finds established in the adult organism may be found spread out and writ large over the earlier history of the organism, just as what is established as species-specific in the individual's development may be found developing in the earlier history of the species. The unconscious, which knows neither time nor death, is the locus in the adult of the forgotten states of experience of infancy.

The displacements of the experience of being overwhelmed by internal stimulation, into forms of registration in which it can be grasped and responded to, are, in the light of the above observations, the beginning of the production of time as salient to the organism's experience. They are also the beginning of the production of the established differentiation between inside and outside, and hence between individual and species, or individual and society, "An infant at the breast does not as yet distinguish his ego from the external world as the source of the sensations flowing in upon him. He must be very strongly impressed by the fact that some sources of excitation... only reappear as a result of his screaming for help."[22]

The outside and the inside, too, receive registrations in which they are salient to the individual organism's experience. The (internal and external) surfaces of the body appear, ultimately, as the ego. The external social reality, its specific organisation, ignorance of which is as much a danger to the organism as any other reality, appears as the super-ego. That which is beyond the bounds of individual and social organisation, which is neither inside nor outside because it pre-exists these differentiations, that which is not accorded the reality conferred by organised knowledge, remains as the id.

All of these differentiating organisations, like any human organisations, including thinking and the acquisition or production of knowledge, come about in the process of development which finds its first marks in the displacements of the experience of traumatic overwhelming which first allow this experience to be grasped in a form which can be handled, a form which is itself the first grasping and handling, the first response.

The possibility of that first displacement, of displacement itself, is most mysterious. The possibility of that displacement is the assumption and rock on which all of psychoanalysis rests. It is the form of representation or registering in which the fact of change from one kind of state into another kind of state first allows itself to be grasped and handled by Freud, a form which is itself the first grasping and handling.

It is the problem of thinking change from one kind of whole to another kind of whole, when all of this is itself a whole. Wholes entire unto themselves need to be thought as parts, and independent parts, being the different wholes, entire unto themselves, need to be thought as parts which depend for their meaning on each other, being parts of a whole entire unto itself, the whole consisting in the change from one kind of a whole to another — or consisting in the relation of one kind of a whole to another, when change is not in the question.

And the possibility of this displacement appears as such in the context of Freud's aim of producing change, in therapeutic analysis, from one state of experience to another state of experience, each highly differentiated from the other, each highly organised, and each connected to the other via the mediation of a passage through the disorganised undifferentiation of the id. Connected on the patient's side by a denial of the id, connected on the analyst's side by an affirmation of the id.[23]

But there are two denials, and two affirmations. There is the denial which is repression, which knows nothing of what it has denied, and the denial which is rejection, which denies in full knowledge. And there is the affirmation which is incorporation, or identification or internalisation, which knows nothing of what it affirms, and there is the affirmation which is acceptance, which affirms in full knowledge.[24] The patient denies in the first way, and affirms, too, in the first way. The analyst affirms and denies, too, but both in the second way. This means that the analyst denies and affirms in full knowledge of the id, that is, in full knowledge of the first ways of denying and affirming, which, since s/he too is a member of the species, are also his or her ways of denying and affirming.

What makes the analyst and her/his relation to the id, and to the unconscious in general, different from the patient and his/her relation to the id and to the unconscious in general, is that the analyst knows, in the second way, that s/he is like the patient, but the patient does not know, in the first way, that s/he is not like the analyst. If the patient knew in the first way that s/he was not like the analyst, then s/he would know in the second way that s/he *was* like the analyst. For Freud's purposes there are two kinds of states of experience, the one analysed and the other unanalysed; these are two forms of organisation, and two forms of knowledge, and it's the interplay of the two forms of knowledge that makes all the difference. "Nothing takes place between them except that they talk to each other.... And incidentally do not let us despise the *word*. After all it is a powerful instrument...."[25]

As for the id, it knows nothing of purposes. "It cannot say what it wants; it has achieved no unified will."[26] It is a play of forces, moving in accordance with compulsions the aggregate tendency of which is described by the principle of constancy. The displaced registrations of the play of forces, however, in the first of which it is represented to itself in the movement towards purposive organisation, these displaced registrations may include purposes, which may then be bandied about in the play of forces, or which may become far enough displaced to map out a purposive space sufficiently extensive to split and displace and reverse some of the compulsions in accordance with *its* own aggregate tendency, to isolate and undo some of them, to ward them off with greater and greater assurance of constant effectiveness, while channelling them in the increasingly organised paths produced by its increasingly complex and differentiated purposes.[27]

As the new displacements progressively make a space in which to organise themselves, they become increasingly independent of the original tendency of the play of forces, and consequently each displaced position is able to proliferate its own network of displacements, having no necessary or internal relation to the preceding and succeeding displacements of the major series. In the context of the species:

> The transformations of scientific opinion are developments, advances, not revolutions. A law which was held at first to be universally valid proves to be a special case of a more comprehensive uniformity, or is limited by another law, not discovered till later....There are various fields where we have not yet surmounted a phase of research in which we make trial with hypotheses that soon have to be rejected as in-

adequate; but in other fields we already possess an assured and almost unalterable core of
knowledge.[28]

The infant does not have a knowledge that is worthy
of the name, since the infant knows neither the limits of its
knowledge nor how to utilise that knowledge, including its
limits, to attain purposes which are other than the aggregate
tendency of the play of forces that constitutes it. At the decisive point at which the infant invaginates on or into itself,
however, producing a number of dynamically opposed organisations of forces, it constitutes two knowledges at a single
stroke, one that is worthy of the name and one that isn't. In
Freud's account, the latter is constituted by the recognition
that loss of the saving object is possible. It's not, in men, that
the salient representative of this loss, the penis, is really taken
away. The primal repression occurs as a result of the recognition that one of the parents does in fact not have a penis,
that it is therefore possible that the pertinent penis was cut
off, and it is in consequence of the importance of this mere
possibility, applied to the boy's own penis, that the repression occurs.

What is thereby fixed, as a permanent assumption, is
that the alternatives are between the penis' being removed
and its not being removed; that is, that the penis, and hence
the saving object as the route to which it is valued, really do
exist with the importance that was wished for in them.[29]

In other words, a possibility is treated as a fact, because it is imperative not to be overwhelmed by internal
excitation, and it is that mistaken decision, that error as to
what in fact happened, that flips the infantile play of forces
in on itself, producing a stable inside and outside, and a
second knowledge which tests possibilities against the real
events of internal and external reality. Freud: "It seems to me
unnecessary for me to appeal here to the 'as if' which has
become so popular. The value of a 'fiction' of this kind...

132

depends on how much one can achieve with its help."[30]

Since this second knowledge presupposes both the stable differentiation of inside and outside, and the connected sucession of time, in which to defer its decisions while not losing the accumulating information and experiences which will allow the decisions ultimately to be made, this second knowledge is only possible after the event of the first. Conversely, we may infer that the constitution of the first knowledge, a knowledge fixed in place and given its orientation by an error, which is also the moment of the constitution of the second knowledge, so that the first knowledge is constituted not *before* the event of the second, and is itself possible only after that event, is made possible by the holding back that gives time to think in the second knowledge.

Each knowledge, considered on its own, as a whole entire unto itself, requires the other to come first. Hence the theory, which is committed to explaining in terms of a whole entire unto itself, and consequently to a whole divided against and external to itself, requires a locus in which time and knowledge worthy of the name are irrelevant: again, the unconscius, or the id, an outside within the whole without which the whole does not, on its own terms, make sense.

In the case of women, the unconscious, in which, so to speak, the id entirely resides, is constituted in consequence of the realisation that the penis has already been removed, that the means to the loving and saving object is already taken away, and the resentment and envy that this incurs in the little girl leads her on a circuitous series of displacements far removed from the original tendency of the play of forces that she was.[31] Her knowledges are also founded on an error; the first knowledge is oriented by the error, the second presupposes the first. The penis was never taken away, there is nothing to resent, invagination is as worthy and necessary as salient projection.

Unfortunately, the second knowledge forgets, with a will, not only that the play of forces exists, but also that the invagination, founded on an error in the eyes of any knowledge worthy of the name, the invagination which constitutes both the play of forces as a knowledge not worthy of the name and also the second knowledge as one which can wait and see—the second knowledge forgets that invagination, too, exists and that without it time, inside and outside, and thinking that occurs in time, could not get under way. Consequently only salient projection is valued in this second knowledge, and not invagination which turns back on or into itself, so that the little girl is right to resent, not the lack of the penis, but the absence of the lack of the penis in the eyes of the second knowledge, the failure of the second knowledge to estimate or recognise this lack at its full foundational value.[32]

The failure to grant the lack the full status of reality: the vagina is not permitted to be salient; the penis is not permitted to be absent; because the penis is not permitted to be absent, and not permitted with such forceful resistance, the possibility that the penis is not absent can never be brought to the light of testing which suspends its conclusions: so that the penis is not permitted not to be absent, either, and it is because of the lack of this possible absence that the vagina is not permitted to be salient in its own right, and not permitted with such force of resistance. The knowledges belonging to the bearers of each of the sexual organs is connected via the mediation of a passage through an absent knowledge, an absent knowledge lacked by each of the bearers insofar as it is not recognised that there is no missing piece, but rather a real missing, a real wanting.

The lack which governs this separation of the two knowledges is the lack of recognition that there is no missing piece. The only lack, which is a real failing, is the lack in recognition of a lack. And it is this error, this mistaken lack of a lack, which is responsible for the reality in human experience of connected successive time. It is this mistaken lack of a lack which provides the room to manoeuvre in order to get what one wants, and which allows thinking and the acquisition or production of knowledge. Should the lack be given full recognition, there would be no more knowledge, only a play of forces and what one wants, what one is wanting, what one lacks.

And then one would mourn, like Hamlet, the only real absence, which is the absence of a real, and not merely a possible, absence.[33] One would mourn not the absence of the penis, but the absence of its absence, which is equivalent to the representation of the absent penis, the phallic signifier, which is the signifier of the mother's penis, which is where it all began.[34]

The saving object, protection against being overwhelmed by internal stimulation, the one who can contain one's discharge and secrete a nourishing lack of stimulation into one; if this object does not lack a lack, and only if this object does not lack a lack, does it have power to save. If it lacks a lack, then it has no nothing to give, and nothing is what is wanted by an organism disintegrating from overfull internal stimulation.

If the mother simply does not have a penis, then nothing is lacking, nothing does not make itself felt, there is nothing not salient which can thereby be salient in the right way to an overfull organism bursting with salient intensities. The error of not recognising the absence is absolutely essential if the vital absence is to be attained, so that time, thinking, will, and the survival that these make possible can take place. The effect of this error is the elaborate institutionalisation of the principle of constancy, the psychological equivalent of which is the pleasure–unpleasure principle.

The organism can't help being alive, since it is already a living play of forces, but it can ensure that that unpleasant fact is kept out of the way. The displacements by which it achieves this forgetful turning against its reality are the displacements which make thinking and the acquisition or production of knowledge possible. The first displacement is the beginning of the change from a play of forces to someone who knows; and knowledge is a compromise formation between the deflected forces and the channels along which they are organised. "We may insist as often as we like that man's intellect is powerless in comparison with his instinctual life, and we may be right in this. Nevertheless, there is something peculiar about this weakness. The voice of the intellect is a soft one, but it does not rest till it has gained a hearing. Finally, after a countless succession of rebuffs, it succeeds."[35]

The point at which the organism turns back on or into itself, at which it invaginates, is the point at which the id is constituted as a knowledge not worthy of the name, and the ego and superego are constituted as knowledges which may be worthy of the name. At that point the crucial displacement which has led to the invagination is constituted as the first step of knowledge.

And also as the first play of forces. It is theory which lets us know that the id consists in forces, and that it itself depends on and is a subtle form of these forces. And these forces, then, are also an unsubtle form of *it*, of knowledge. Because theory requires us to say that it is no more than a play of forces, it also requires us to say that these forces are no less than a theoretical knowledge. The commitment to thinking in terms of a whole entire unto itself requires the simultaneous thinking in two independent logics, of two independent kinds of thing.

The first step of knowledge is the error of lacking recognition of a lack. The possibility of taking the first step of knowledge is the possibility of displacement. The possibility of displacement is therefore the possibility of the error of lacking recognition of a lack, the possibility of the absence of an absence of an absence.

Knowledge, and with it the organism, in the end catches itself from behind:

A further characteristic of obsessional neurosis,

as of all similar affections, is that its manifesta-
tions (its symptoms, including the obsessive
actions) fulfil the condition of being a compromise between the warring forces of the mind.
They thus always reproduce something of the
pleasure which they are designed to prevent;
they serve the repressed instinct no less than
the agencies which are repressing it. As the illness progresses, indeed, actions which were
originally mostly concerned with maintaining
the defence come to approximate more and
more to the proscribed actions through which
the instinct was able to find expression in childhood.[36]

The first step of knowledge which is worthy of the
name, is the absence of the lack of a gap, an absence which
preceded the lack of a gap of which it is an absence, and a
lack which preceded the gap of which it is a lack, so that the
gap can be there despite the fact that it is lacking, and the
lack of the gap can be there despite the fact that it is absent,
and the absence, which has nothing to support it, cannot be
there at all, so that it is the only real lack, the only real
failing.

This is all impossible; nonetheless, back to front and
upside down as it is, the possible, including time and the
possibility of knowledge which is worthy of the name, is
founded on it. The primal repression takes a gap from which
something is not absent and, with great force, refuses to recognise that gap from which something is not absent. It insists on recognising it as a gap from which something *is*
absent, and in that way it has a spare "not" to play around
with, a little piece of absence smuggled into the play of forces:
"it would after all be right and proper to describe repression,
which lies at the basis of every neurosis, as a reaction to a
trauma — as an elementary traumatic neurosis."[37]

137

The compulsions of the play of forces know nothing about "not," or about absence. They know only about incorporation or expulsion. But now it's a question of the expulsion of an expulsion which has been expelled: the lack which wasn't recognised, the recognition which failed in consequence of an error, and the error which must disappear because it depends on not being an error in order to be as precise an error as it is. All the play of forces can do is to go round in circles that never close on themselves, for which there is no beginning and no end, and no inside which does not become an outside. In short, it invaginates, and is a perpetual invagination, forever differing from itself, forever deferring itself. For "we never can relinquish anything; we only exchange one thing for something else. When we appear to give something up, all we really do is to adopt a substitute."[38]

This play of forces is only one of the details of the working of the idea of the unconscious: it serves only to give a clue as to the nature of the logic of thinking things through as a whole, entire unto itself. Neither the word "play" nor the word "force" means what it might otherwise mean.

But in the spaces created by the circular movements there are displacements which can follow the organisation of knowledge and the connected succession of time that goes with it. "We can avoid any possible abuse of this method of representation by recollecting that ideas, thoughts and psychical structures in general must never be regarded as localized in organic elements of the nervous system but rather, as one might say, *between* them, where resistances and facilitations... provide the corresponding correlates. Everything that can be an object of our internal perception is *virtual*...."[39] A gap has been created in which waiting can occur, and the gap has been created, where a gap was lacking, by turning the lack of the gap, itself, in the decisive end, against itself, against the lack of the gap. The lack of the gap recognised itself, but not as the lack of the gap, and in that way it created a gap.

And these spaces, lacks, and gaps, too, are only details of the working of the logic of thinking things through as a whole. These words have their meaning only in giving a clue to the nature of that logic.

At this point, at which for the first time it is possible to say something, there is only nothing to be said. This is where one has, for the first time, arrived: at nothing, which is not something, but which, on the other hand, for an organism too full of excitation, is not nothing either. There is nothing to be said; there is only what one wants, what one is wanting, what one lacks. And what one wants is, precisely, nothing, a nothing which is neither something nor nothing. And the registrations which this not nothing that is wanted has displaced itself into or on to, in the forms of which it can be grasped and handled, and which are themselves forms of grasping and handling it, already responses to it, these registrations are the breast, a look, the penis, babies, mother, father. These are not the not nothing that they represent or are equivalent to. They are, precisely, not not nothings.

What one wants, which one can say, is one or another not not nothing. And this is how time extends itself, within which thinking can occur, climbing up on a support, and then removing that support to place it elsewhere, further along towards where one wants to go, or further towards what one wants to say. The unconscious, in which there is no time, and no purpose, knows no "no," either.

The achievement of the function of judgment only becomes feasible, however, after the creation of the symbol of negation has endowed thought with a first degree of independence from the results of repression and at the same time from the sway of the pleasure principle.

This view of negation harmonizes very well with the fact that in analysis we never discover

a "No" in the unconscious, and that a recognition of the unconscious on the part of the ego is
expressed an a negative formula.[40]

But time, in the realm of the knowledge which contains negation, is endless, because one can never say the nothing that
one wants; and that, ultimately, is all that one ever wants, so
that one has to carry on seeking, or asking questions, anyway.

The play of forces knows nothing of values or choices;
it simply does what it does, without asking questions. The
displaced registrations of the play of forces, however, in which
it represents itself to itself, may be questions or choices or
values. And, indeed, what is taken in when the organism
fails to recognise in itself the same lack of a gap that it fails to
recognise in its mother, what is remodelled in the ego which
constitutes it as able to help itself in the way the parents can,
is the parental power in the social organisation of reality,
their command of values which becomes the command of
the super-ego.[41] That is, when the play of forces invaginates,
it becomes an individual organism which bears within its
organisation the purposes and directions entailed in the ad-
herence to social values. That is, values are now fact as far as
the efficient working of the principle of constancy, the tendency to a lowering of internal levels of stimulation is concerned. A failure to obey those values leads to anxiety, guilt,
or pain, forms of unpleasure which are the psychological
registering of the violation of the constancy principle. Values
have become an integral part of the functioning of the constellations of forces.

In fact, since, in the whole entire unto itself which
Freud is trying to explain, the parts all depend on each other
for their meaning, the meaning of forces, considered as all
there is, entire unto itself, is given by everything that is *not*
forces, considered as entire unto itself, that is, without any
reference to forces at all. In other words, the moment Freud

finds truth in drives and forces to the exclusion of everything else, he *also* finds truth in such things as values, commitments, meanings and purposes, to the exclusion of such
things as drives and forces.

The unconscious, or the id, is not a collection of forces:
from the beginning, to the extent that it is a collection of
forces, it is a collection of meanings, values and aspirations
considered without reference to forces. The unconscious and
the id are ways of talking about thinking things through as a
whole; and the particular terms Freud chose through which
to conduct this thinking are irrelevant to his achievement, if
not to his location in history and culture and to his personal
preferences. His achievement lies in conducting this thinking, superbly and skilfully, with truth to its rigorous requirements, its logic. It is all the more of an achievement in that he
conducted it through terms perhaps badly suited to it.

Furthermore — to continue— the invagination creates
a nothing to supply the lack of a cessation of stimulation that
the organism is wanting, and at the same stroke it does away
with the lack of this cessation, so that the organism no longer
wants the nothing since now it has it. The organism now has
its own nothing to say, and, gradually, as time proceeds, it
displaces this onto or into a proliferation of not not nothings,
which it thinks are quite something. And, by human stan-
dards, it is quite correct, since these not not nothings are the
linchpins of the constellations of the forces that constitute it,
in the form of the values which flipped into the organism's
functioning when it involuted in the act of becoming its own
saving object.

> Civilisation is the fruit of renunciation
> of instinctual satisfaction, and from each new-
> comer in turn it exacts the same renunciation....
> In the last resort it may be said that every inter-
> nal compulsion which has been of service in
> the development of human beings was origi-

nally, that is, in the evolution of the human race, nothing but an external one. Those who are born today bring with them as an inherited constitution some degree of a tendency (disposition) towards transmutation of egoistic into social instincts... And so the human being is subject not only to the pressure of his immediate environment, but also to the influence of the cultural development attained by his forefathers.[42]

Consequently the organism can develop a knowledge worthy of the name, which is not not nothing, or quite something, because it satisfies the organism very deeply, feeding the constancy principle with a superabundance of not not nothings. From which we may infer that the distinction is not between knowledge pertinent to the workings of nature and knowledge pertinent to human concerns, but between knowledge that does as it pleases well, and knowledge that does as it pleases badly, each of the latter pair including both of the former pair.

The difference between these two knowledges, according to Freud, who was good at knowledge, is that the knowledge that does as it pleases well knows, in the sense of rejection and acceptance, that it is like the knowledge that does as it pleases badly; while the knowledge that does as it pleases badly does not know, in the sense of repression and internalisation, that it is not like the knowledge that does as it pleases well. If it did know, in the sense of repression and internalisation, that it was not like the knowledge that does as it pleases well, it would know, in the sense of rejection and acceptance, that it was like the knowledge that does as it pleases well.

For Freud's purposes, there are two kinds of states of experience, the one analysed, and the other unanalysed: these are two forms of organisation, and two forms of knowledge, and it's the interplay of the two forms of knowledge that makes all the difference. The analyst is able to find his/her satisfaction without recourse to an external saving object. The patient is unable to find such satisfaction, which is why s/he has come to the analyst.

In the analytic situation, in which there are two human beings, there are four knowledges in play with and against one another. The same applies to reading a book, most pertinently to reading Freud's books. Freud is dead, the consummation devoutly to be wished, but his dreams live on. The organism desires silently to die, Freud tells us, to return to its former inorganic state, and at the same time it desires noisily to bind its world into ever larger unities to restore its primary undifferentiation by the long route. It lacks a lack: it lacks the lack of itself. It takes a short cut to creating this lack of a lack by failing to recognise itself. This looks like the long route because the end is already accomplished at the beginning.

The subject of the knowledge worthy of the name is already dead, already beyond the whole or at the limits of the whole itself. The decision to think of things as a whole, entire unto itself, when rigorously followed through, leads to this understanding, contains this detail already within it, as part of what it itself means, as a whole. The subject of the knowledge which is not worthy of the name is the same subject, split down the middle by the same stroke which, invaginating, created the two knowledges. The subject of these two knowledges plays with her/himself. S/he wets his/her bed, s/he drops out of sight in the not not nothing that is the knowledge worthy of the name, and s/he displays him/herself to her/himself in the hieroglyphs of the dreams that line her/his pyramid of solitary sleep.

The subject of knowledge found the nothing that s/he wants, and consequently no longer wants it. S/he walks in the graveyards, surveying the ruins and decayed remnants of Michelangelo and Leonardo da Vinci, Shakespeare and

Dostoyevski, Plato, Empedocles and Kant. The death drive need be nothing but silent: it has accomplished its purpose in advance, in the first step the play of forces took to become its own saving object. The first step of knowledge, good and evil, was the last step of life. The rest is history, occurring between the first and last limits of the whole, which is what it is by having given those limits and that beyond meaning only within itself, so that what is not subject to history, what is beyond the time within the whole, is now a beyond which is within, a not which is within, a not-conscious which is nonetheless part of mental life: an unconscious.[43]

The life drive, Eros, must needs be noisy; like Falstaff, it has already lost; but it was never anything but a substitute for, a displacement of, the death drive, in accordance with the principle of constancy. Eros is the form in which Thanatos represents itself to itself, registers itself in a form that can be grasped and dealt with. Eros is the principle of the lack of a lack of a lack, which is not not nothing. Thanatos is the principle of the lack of a lack, the lack of a lack of itself, which is not nothing, but it is not something, either. Thanatos hides behind Freud's text, behind his discourse; Eros is death's way of hiding, the noisy absence of death.

Life, according to Freud, is made up of the interplay and interfusion of Eros and Thanatos. Life includes life and death. The play of all the parts of the whole includes both the play of all the parts and what is beyond or at the limits of the whole itself. But the subject is never more dead than when s/he is most noisily awake, and never more alive than in the silent tomb of dreaming sleep. Heraclitus: awake, all I see is death; asleep, dreams. The place of life in knowledge is neither here nor there. The subject of knowledge is the ghost of the dead fathers, in whose names the values of the social order are made into a linchpin of the functioning of the constellation of forces that constitute the individual organism.

His early symptom of death-like seizures can

thus be understood as a father-identification on the part of his ego, permitted by his super-ego as a punishment. "You wanted to kill your father in order to be your father yourself. Now you *are* your father, but a dead father" — the regular mechanism of hysterical symptoms. And further, "Now your father is killing *you*."... Both of them, the ego and the super-ego, carry on the role of the father.

To sum up, the relation between the subject and his father-object, while retaining its content, has been transformed into a relation between the ego and the super-ego — a new setting on a fresh stage.[44]

The invagination which produces the organism as an individual at the same time sacrifices its idiosyncrasies to the reproductive and self-protective purposes of the species.[45]

Put the other way round, the invagination which sacrifices the idiosyncracies of the organism to the requirements of the species at the same time produces the organism as an individual, and produces a species capable of having requirements considered independently of the individual.

But what we are now in a position to note is that the theory which allows us to articulate this invagination is itself the product of an invagination, as we must recognise if we think this self-referential theory through properly. That is, the very theory which most demonstrates the self-conflict inherent in the character of being human also demonstrates — depends on — the unconflicted independence of the two sides of the conflict, as wholes unto themselves, since it is the inescapability of this self-conflicted logic which the theory demonstrates.

That is, what Freud shows us how to think is, *simultaneously*, the conflictual connection between individual and society, each partly finding the meaning of what it *is* in the other, *and* the simple independence of each to the other, each being able to see the other entirely from the outside. Similarly with the history by which we, individually and socially, became what we are, and the present state in which we exist as what we are. And similarly with ideals and aspirations versus drives.

This extraordinarily vital and fruitful contribution was what Jung missed, in his entirely crude division of the unconscious into collective and personal. Freud thought this either/or as *both* an either/or *and* /(*and/or*) /*or* a both/and, in *one* way of thinking, summarised for us in the idea of the Freudian unconscious.

With the idea of the unconscious Freud showed a way of remaining committed to the inside of one's thinking and understanding without thereby being unable to understand outside of it. He showed a way of taking responsibility for one's point of view, in the senses both of being responsible *to* it and being responsible *for* it.

Differently put, the idea of the unconscious, and the kind of thinking and exploration that go with it, allow us to establish what we *can* take responsibility for and what we can't, what we are unfair to take responsibility for within us, and what it is unfair not to take responsibility for, outside us. And this in a way strictly to be re-evaluated from time to time.

Death is larger than life; it looms behind and embraces life in the comforting shadow of its brooding wings. It says, with Keats, already with thee, tender is the night. Eros is death's way of accomplishing its task, the absence of the lack of the lack of itself. Death includes life and death. This was Freud's contribution to the task of knowledge, but he was of course too modest to acknowledge, even to himself, so momentous a contribution to the workings of human destiny. It did, however, satisfy him very deeply, in accordance with the accuracy of his knowledge of the principle of constancy, the pleasure-unpleasure principle.

This is also why the Oedipal resolution and the entry into knowledge is properly a mourning. One mourns the possible absence of an absence, so as to make it truly gone, then it is the absence of the possible absence of an absence. One mourns in order to establish death, so that life can go on, afterwards. Before the mourning, life included death; after the mourning, death includes life. Then one is in a position to choose, with efficacious long-term will, what life one wishes to lead. Before that one is too busy trying to die to have time to choose. And

> mourning has a quite specific psychical task to perform: its function is to detach the survivors' memories and hopes from the dead. When this has been achieved, the pain grows less and with it the remorse and self-reproaches and consequently the fear of the demon as well. And the same spirits who to begin with were feared as demons may now expect to meet with friendlier treatment; they are revered as ancestors and appeals are made to them for help.[46]

If one has died once, one knows at least that one can do it again. But only if one has done it properly the first time. And one can only do that by taking the saving object, the lack of the lack of the lack, inside one, identifying with it, so that it can kill one from within, undoing the crime, the transgression against the constancy principle, which life is, so that one can get one's revenge by haunting it, and rattling the chains of Eros.

In short, Freud does three profound and important things. Firstly, he shows how, by thinking from the point of view of the whole of things, the limit and boundary of knowledge — which he thinks in terms of death — what is within that whole — life — is revealed in relation to that whole; and vice-versa; and how thinking from each of these points of

147

view *is* thinking from the other: and by this division of the whole of our understanding against itself, he shows us how to move from one whole understanding to another, since a whole understanding divided against itself is the same as two whole understandings at one with each other, each, in Heraclitus' phrase, living in the other's death.

Secondly, he shows how to take responsibility for the part our knowledge, our taken for granted assumptions, classifications and categories by which we divide up our world(s), plays in giving it the meaning(s) it has for us. By focusing consistently on the contribution of our knowledge, he reveals consistently the contribution made by what we *don't* know, by what is not knowledge or affected by knowledge, what he calls, variously, heredity or anatomy or necessity (*Ananke*).

And, thirdly, he shows how these two things are also divided against and one with each other. Reason, or knowledge, and necessity, thought each from its own independent point of view, *are* thought from the point of view of their indivisible unity, the identity, in Parmenides' phrase, of thinking and being. This indivisible unity, including the unity of, on the one hand, indivisible unity itself and, on the other, division against self, is what he calls, variously, the it, or the unconscious, or instinctual representatives, the always already displaced forces of one's disposition.

To take responsibility for one's knowledge, in order to change, and as a result of changing, one's whole understanding of a particular issue, is to accept, for that time of taking responsibility and changing, that it as being I, including the acceptance of rejection, of the non-acceptance with which one begins, the it as definitely not I. The suffering of the knowledge of life, says the Chorus of Sophocles' *King Oedipus*, "must needs be borne/Twice; once in the body and once in the soul"; and the lesson of the tragedy, they say, is "that mortal man must always look to his ending."[47] This acceptance goes through the movement Freud's thought shows,

each stage with its own accurate vocabulary and syntax: first
the acceptance of the split between reason and instinct; then
the acceptance that one's reason gives one's instinctual representatives their meaning — it is one's particular life which
makes one's death what it is, one's resolved issues which
haunt one's ghosts; then, the acceptance that one's instinctual representatives give one's reason the force it has for one;
then, finally, the acceptance of the split between instinct or
drive, as one form of knowledge and force, and reason, as
another form of knowledge and force, each operating in its
own way, and the two unified, divided, mutually transfor-
mative, and mutually independent, in the ways they happen
to be. Freud, who is perhaps best compared with Pascal, was
a great practising logician, which is nowhere more clearly
evident than in the careful inconsistency of of his terminol-
ogy and metaphors. As Wittgenstein wrote:

If the good or bad exercise of the will
does alter the world, it can alter only the limits
of the world, not the facts — not what can be
expressed by means of language.
In short the effect must be that it becomes
an altogether different world. It must, so to
speak, wax and wane as a whole.
The world of the happy man is a different one from that of the unhappy man.[48]

The fact is, however, that Freud was able to bring the
place of death, of the limits of life and knowledge as a whole,
out into the open, and to incorporate it into his knowledge of
the knowledge that does as it pleases well, and the knowledge that does as it pleases badly. This suggests that death
has done its work so thoroughly, that the idiosyncrasy of the
individual organism is so thoroughly subordinated in species-specific, typical development to the reproductive purposes of society, that death and knowledge no longer need

to hide in order to be effectively established. The development of material conditions must have played their part in
producing Freud and his widespread influence; Western civilisation must be ripe for the open affirmation — in the sense
of incorporation or identification and not necessarily of acceptance — of death.

> In former times it was different. Then utter-
> ances such as mine brought with them a sure
> curtailment of one's earthly existence and an
> effective speeding-up of the opportunity for
> gaining a personal experience of the after-life.
> But, I repeat, those times are past and to-day
> writings such as this bring no more danger to
> their author than to their readers.[49]

This is not the death of values. On the contrary, it is
the total victory of values, as registered in the commands of
the super-ego. Guilt and mourning are very closely related.[50]
But it is the death of the lack of death. It is the end of the
drive to bind the world in ever greater unities, which ends
because it has succeeded in its task. It means that the patient
can say to Freud the nothing that s/he has to say, and mourn
again, mourn his/her previous mourning, establishing the
death of what s/he was before, and choosing idiosyncratic
values. And it means that Freud can know that what the
patient wants is nothing, so that he can offer it to him/her,
making a space and a time for the patient to retrace her/his
path of not not nothings, until s/he gets to his/her not nothing which s/he can recognise, making a new not not nothing
from the position of which s/he can mourn, so that s/he can
choose and proliferate a new path of not not nothings, and in
that way do as s/he pleases well. Heraclitus: the way up and
the way down are the same, but the way up is better.
In the end the patient knows, in the sense of acceptance and rejection, that s/he, like the analyst, has or is two

knowledges, that s/he can play with her/himself if s/he pleases, and that that is not not nothing—indeed, quite something.

Death wins by losing; Eros loses by winning. And this means a great deal more. It means, in the eyes of any knowledge worthy of the name, that the constellation of forces which constitutes human society as a whole, which society knows in the sense of identification and repression,[51] has achieved the aim of its aggregate tendency. Consequently the individual organism contains in the form and structuring of its registrations or inscriptions the functioning of an entire species, entire in the sense that it has completed the life cycle which it was internally driven to map out or circumscribe; "what we have isolated as individual psychology, by neglecting all traces of the group, has only since come into prominence out of the old group psychology, by a gradual process which may still, perhaps, be described as incomplete."[52] There is no longer, therefore, a necessity, in the eyes of any knowledge worthy of the name, to postulate internal connections between individual and species.

And Freud's analysis operates in that knowledge: the analyst reflects the patient like a mirror, only because the analyst is capable of being truly outside the patient. The analyst is capable of playing dead so that, in effect, s/he is, from the point of view of the knowledge salient to the patient, the knowledge of identification and repression, which is not a knowledge worthy of the name, which is why it insists on postulating internal connections.

But there is more. The subject which formerly could not be recognised, because then it would know that it was alive, the horror of horrors in accordance with the constancy principle, can now be recognised and recognise itself, in the simple act of recognising itself as to be recognised as not recognised. The lack of a lack, the non-recognition of a recognition as not recognised, has become the absence of a lack of a lack. In accordance with the constancy principle, this can only mean that the lack of a lack, the status of the former subject, is already absent, the former subject is already dead. It is therefore now recognised in a life after death.

And more. The knowledge, the recognition which puts the final touch on the death of the subject, is itself of a piece with the constellation of forces in whose workings it has become so integral a part in comparison with the more primitive stages of the history of the species. It is the most refined, least intense part of the constellation of forces.[53] And since the possibility of displacement is, in the terms of the workings of the organised force that we call knowledge and thinking, the possibility of the error of lacking recognition of a lack, the workings of knowledge, of error and accuracy, are themselves the underpinnings of the possibility of change from one state of experience to another state of experience, including the possibility of invagination, and the possibility of the emergence of life from an inorganic state.

This ties in with Freud's statement that :

The problem would seem even more difficult if we had to admit that mental impulses could be so completely suppressed as to leave no trace whatever behind them. But that is not the case. Even the most ruthless suppression must leave room for distorted surrogate impulses and for reactions resulting from them. If so, however, we may safely assume that no generation is able to conceal any of its more important mental processes from its successor. For psychoanalysis has shown us that everyone possesses in his unconscious mental activity an apparatus which enables him to interpret other people's reactions, that is, to undo the distortions which other people have imposed on the expression of their feelings. An unconscious understanding such as this of all the customs, ceremonies and dog-

mas left behind by the original relation to the
father may have made it possible for later gen-
erations to take over their heritage of emotion.[54]

Nature or the cosmos knows no purposes and no
knowledge. But there is no knowledge worthy of the name,
knowledge which recognises the absence of the saving object, the absence of the god who founds knowledge outside
human concerns, which does not ascribe purposes and the
knowledge in which they find their possibility and their context to nature and the cosmos.

The fact that knowledge and the values it presupposes
and is presupposed by have closed the life cycle of the species is evident in the possibility of discovering the logical
articulation, the algorithm of pure abstract functioning, of
the invagination which decisively introduces the organism
to the heritage of its species, the resolution of the Oedipal
complex. This algorithm, the workings presupposed by the
first displacement by which the organism registered itself in
itself, is the absence of recognition of the lack of a lack. And
when the analysis brings the subject to a reworking of this
invagination, the algorithm becomes the recognised error of
failing to recognise the lack of a lack, which immediately
displaces the subject elsewhere, into the new position in which
s/he recognises; and it allows by this displacement the cu-
mulatively stabilising realignment of the registrations in virtue of which the organism is organised and disorganised in
the ways it is.

And here the theory has invaginated again. By coming to the point at which the history of the species is understood to be complete in the individual, one has also come to
a position in which that understanding of a whole entire
unto itself is the means of making itself insufficient, the means
of opening up a new position which needs to be thought
through entirely in its own terms, and from which the former understanding, which led to the latter by closing off all

avenues from itself, can be seen from the outside.

The fourth step, the recognition of the error, disappears as salient to the organism as soon as the organism has proliferated its registrations sufficiently in their new path, so that the absence of recognition of lack of a lack supervenes, and the hiatus of the error rejoins the lack of a lack to complete the mourning for death, thereby accomplishing it again. The error, the missing fourth step, is the tomb of death and the cornerstone of life. It is the latter in the form of the missing piece for which Eros, the play of the parts of the whole striving to become unified, restlessly yearns.

I anticipate: "If we had to do with a dream, it would at once occur to us that caskets are also women, symbols of the essential thing in woman, and therefore of a woman herself, like boxes, large or small, baskets, and so on."[55] And

> the Hours... became guardians of the law of Nature, and of the divine order of things whereby the constant recurrence of the same things in unalterable succession in the natural world takes place.
>
> This knowledge of nature reacted on the conception of human life. The nature-myth changed into a myth of human life: the weather-goddesses became goddesses of destiny.... The implacable severity of this law, the affinity of it with death and ruin, avoided in the winsome figures of the Hours, was now stamped upon the Moerae, as though mankind had only perceived the full solemnity of natural law when he had to submit his own personality to its working.[56]

I would draw attention to the full resonances of the word "conception" above, and to the processual sense they make independently and in mutual relation. Finally, in a second reversal:

> Against this subjection something in man was
> bound to struggle, for it is only with extreme
> unwillingness that he gives up his claim to an
> exceptional position.... So his imagination re-
> belled against the recognition of the truth em-
> bodied in the myth of the Moerae, and con-
> structed instead the myth derived from it, in
> which the Goddess of Death was replaced by
> the Goddess of Love and by that which most
> resembles her in human shape...
> ...the replacement by the wish-opposite of
> which we have spoken in our theme is built
> upon an ancient identity.
> ...A wished-for reversal is again found here.
> Choice stands in the place of necessity, of des-
> tiny. Thus man overcomes death, which in
> thought he has acknowledged. No greater
> triumph of wish-fulfilment is conceivable. Just
> where in reality he obeys compulsion, he exer-
> cises choice; and that which he chooses is not a
> thing of horror, but the fairest and most desir-
> able thing in life.[57]

In an account of the logic of wish-fulfillment, of drive,
Freud displays the logic which his theory — which allows
this kind of account of its subject matter — requires us to
find both in this theory and the accounts which it allows,
themselves, since they are subtle derivatives of precisely such
drives.

The difference lies in the fact that the theorist or analyst is willing and able, thanks to Freud's development of
this theory and procedure, to pay attention to her/his thought
as potential wish-fulfillment, and consequently as potentially
not wish-fulfillment, because *that* theory can also, on the same

grounds, be wish-fulfillment.

Truth is discoverable by situating oneself firmly in the invagination itself and proceeding tentatively and carefully between two knowledges. The bias of one knowledge or play of forces is overcome by situating one's thinking between the biases of two knowledges or plays of forces. And *this* is done by moving, successively and simultaneously, in each of them.

One's own wishes, then, come to light, and, with the possibility of recognising them, one has the possibility of investigating one's subject matter in ways which will have no reference to them.

The trick is that, to recognise the bias of one's wishes and desires, one has first to investigate without attempting to recognise them, so that they can *fully* direct one, and so emerge plainly. *Then* one investigates the bias one's investigation itself shows. One recognises one's wishes, then, by investigating one's subject matter, and one's subject matter by investigating one's wishes, back and forth.

With the idea of the unconscious and the consequences which flow from it, however, we are dealing, not with knowledge, but with the conditions of its possibility.

And more. In the knowledge which occurs after the invagination, in the thinking which occurs in connected successive time, life includes death, death is an event which occurs at a point in time, and one can ask questions about a life which occurs after that point. In the knowledge which finds its place before the invagination, which is not worthy of the name, death includes life, death is not an event but an operative and effective principle towards the consummation of which life itself tends, and there can be no question of an after death; death is the horizon within which all knowledge finds its possibility. This is the knowledge which Freud has brought into the realm of the knowledge that occurs in time. Freud has bastardised the knowledge worthy of the name by inseminating it with the knowledge not worthy of the name. "The position was at once alarming and consoling, alarming because it was no small thing to have the whole human race as one's patient, and consoling because after all everything was taking place as the premises laid down by psychoanalysis declared that it was bound to."[58]

Freud did not make this as explicit as Heidegger did; but Heidegger lost the radical disparity of the two knowledges simply by virtue of the thoroughness and rigour with which he transformed the one into the other.

Freud, in the same act of bastardisation, has found a way in which two knowledges, each of which, from within its own purview, includes the other, can have a dialogue in which each becomes salient to the other precisely as it intends to from within its own purview. That is to say, since each knowledge operates on the principle that its founding values and principles include those of the other, each of them, in order to communicate as it intends, must begin by communicating its founding principles and values, that which is least recognised by the other, that is, must be able to start before its own beginning. And each does that impossible thing by warping and distorting the language of the other. It emerges that communication between two different loci may in itself always already have operated on the basis of external relations.

And more. What is called life, in the knowledge that follows the invagination, is the death that was sought before the invagination. The epoch that is decisively marked by Freud is the completion of this death, so that what was sought before the invagination can now come out in the open.

> Why do our relatives, the animals, not exhibit
> any such cultural struggle? We do not know....
> It may be that in primitive man a fresh access
> of libido kindled a renewed burst of activity on
> the part of the destructive instinct. There are a
> great many questions here to which as yet there
> is no answer.[59]

157

The skeleton is out of the closet. The life that follows the invagination is now the life of this skeleton, for which the life that precedes the invagination is death. And the two knowledges which register these lives and deaths, the two knowledges which are each ways or forms in which the organism represents itself to itself, and in the interplay of which it has achieved the cycle of its innermost, ownmost aims, so that these aims can be read in that interplay, these two knowledges, each of which includes the other, now co-exist out in the open, and can communicate with each other by means of that very interplay by which the completion of their aims was achieved. There are two forms of life, and two forms of death, and both are salient to the life of the organism in both of its domains of knowledge.

The willingness to enter into the equally salient inter-interplay of both domains of knowledge is what distinguishes the analyst from the patient, and is what characterises analytic practice and the way in which the analyst does as s/he pleases well, in accordance with the values which are now more than ever an integral part of the workings of the two knowledges, or the two systems of forces. These systems of forces are now, for the first time, fully knowledges; this is evident in the fact that for the first time they can represent themselves fully to themselves, that they need no longer catch themselves behind their own backs. The act of baring their logic of operation is at the same time the act of constituting their operation as a logic. Freud has completed the invagination by invaginating it, so that what is most hidden, the taboos and gods and mysteries of the earlier history of the species and of the individual, is now able to be out in the open; and what was most open, the workings of knowledge, is now also the most hidden and surprising.[60]

The invagination which gradually developed over the history of the species, in the context of the time available to and presupposed by the knowledge worthy of the name, is now, in the act of a terminal invagination inaugurated by Freud, turned at right angles to be simultaneous with its own development in the individual, in the knowledge that is not worthy of the name. This knowledge does not occur in time. It occurs in a series, without beginning and without end, of broken rings, a logical rather than a temporal series, in which time, and the life in time, are produced. It is the knowledge of dreams, and jokes, and accidents. But this knowledge also occurs, now that the invagination is itself invaginated, in the context of the knowledge that is worthy of the name, so that the no time, or all of time which it could equally well be said to be, and the life to which no time is salient, occur within the context of connected time, of history. Death occurs within life, and life occurs within death, and vice-versa, and vice-versa.[61]

There is one knowledge that has its legitimate historical origin in another knowledge that, unworthy of the name, has no legitimate origin, no origin that does not begin in the wrong place. The subject of the former knowledge is as dead as dead can be. The subject of the latter knowledge, which is the same subject, invaginated, is fully alive only when it is dead. The subject of the two knowledges, invaginated twice, is neither here nor there, is inside and/(and/or)/or outside, is in time and/ (and/or)/ or too early or too late, in the same act, is an ethical practitioner of analysis.

> For analysis does not undo the *effects* of repression. The instincts which were formerly suppressed remain suppressed; but the same effect is produced in a different way. Analysis replaces the process of repression, which is an automatic and excessive one, by a temperate and purposeful control on the part of the highest agencies of the mind. In a word, *analysis replaces repression by condemnation.* This seems to bring us the long-looked-for evidence that consciousness has

a biological function, and that with its entrance upon the scene an important advantage is secured.[62]

There is one knowledge which has no legitimate origin in another knowledge that is worthy of the name, and that confers legitimacy on the absence of origin, on the one who has no name, and allows that one to revalue the values that are the heritage from the names of the dead fathers. The imperatives of this are, in the same breath, *amor fati*, and the yearning of Zarathustra for a brother who will recognise the way of the one who revalues values.[63]

> The communal life of human beings had, therefore, a two-fold foundation: the compulsion to work, which was created by external necessity, and the power of love, which made the man unwilling to be deprived of his sexual object — the woman—, and made the woman unwilling to be deprived of the part of herself which had been separated off from her — her child. Eros and Ananke (Love and Necessity) have become the parents of human civilization too.[64]

Knowledge plays with its twin by external relations in which the internal relations find their context; but in the eyes of the knowledge worthy of the name, external relations occur in the context of internal relations, so that only half of the game can be played by playing with oneself. This is why Zarathustra has to come down from the mountain; he is full to overflowing, and that, too, is a death.

Time, says Heraclitus, is a child at play. Now there are two times, each the ghost of the other, each seeking recognition from the other, and each, with Freud's analysis, able to recognise the other, and recognise the other correctly, as to be recognised as unrecognised. Then the game can begin, at the beginning and not before the beginning, and with four players for every two people.[65]

What Freud speaks of as the drive to life is what is generally considered to be the drive to death: it seeks to keep excitation low. What Freud uncovers beyond this, which he calls the drive to death, is what is generally considered to be the drive to life: it seeks to repeat itself endlessly. This means that what we mean — in the context of a knowledge and its values that are more than ever an integral part of the workings of the constellation of forces that we are, so that what we mean is of fundamental importance to the way we are — what we mean by life and death, and by a commitment to life and death, is the reverse of what we generally think it means. Since it is only the reverse on the basis of the knowledge which we generally have, since this reversal emerges from the development of the knowledge which is worthy of the name, it is only the reverse on the basis of the truth of what we generally think life and death to mean. Both what we generally think life and death to mean and the reversal of that are therefore true, in their respective domains. But both domains are equally out in the open and equally surprising, equally hidden, and therefore equally important to the way we are.[66]

In other words, the death which Freud signals is the real emergence of the life which originally could not be tolerated, now that the organism is able to help itself, to supply its own lack, its own not not nothing, without depending on the workings of its contemporary species. It needs the species to satisfy its needs, but it can do without it, as the possibility of the revaluation of values that occurs in analysis shows, for quite some time when it comes to the fundamental workings of its own workings, the workings of its desire. The fundamental issue is no longer castration, but the handling of value-laden intensity, of the power that is knowledge. No longer an issue, that is, of recognising and accepting the fact that one is limited in the ways in which one is, but of living life within one's limits, and finding satisfaction with other parts, within the whole as it is, which includes the possibility of being other than it is, over time.

The dead subject, whose death Freud completes by remarking on it, is the originally alive subject, able to live, for the first time, now that sufficient time has passed for a means to develop by which it is known — by which it can come to know — that it can be killed; and since this knowledge has become, in the same passage of time, integral to the workings of this subject, it knows that it is safe to emerge, that the urgency of its demise is not so great that it cannot be tolerated even for an instant. Freud speaks of "the probability that *the psychical impulses of primitive peoples were characterized by a higher amount of ambivalence than is to be found in modern civilized man. It is to be supposed that as this ambivalence diminished, taboo (a symptom of the ambivalence and a compromise between the two conflicting impulses) slowly disappeared."* [67]

Thanatos is the form in which Eros represents itself to itself as already accomplished, which seeks merely to repeat itself as though the first act were sufficient to reach its aim. Eros is the form in which Thanatos represents itself to itself as already accomplished, which seeks to bind as though there were no longer a necessity to die. Each is the accomplishment in advance, too early and too late, of the other. The connecting and binding is therefore the everyday appearance of Thanatos, generally called life and love; the endless repetition, compulsively, of broken rings is the everyday appearance of Eros, generally called death and stagnation. We may compare the following in this regard: "social feeling is based upon the reversal of what was first a hostile feeling into a positively-toned tie in the nature of an identification." [68] And "even to-day the social feelings arise in the individual as a superstructure built upon impulses of jealous rivalry against his brothers and sisters." [69] And

We have treated the difficulty of cultural de-

velopment as a general difficulty of development by tracing it to the inertia of the libido, to
its disinclination to give up an old position for
a new one. We are saying much the same thing
when we derive the antithesis between civilization and sexuality from the circumstance that
sexual love is a relationship between two individuals in which a third can only be superfluous or disturbing, whereas civilization depends
on relationships between a considerable number of individuals. When a love-relationship is
at its height there is no room left for any interest in the environment... In no other case does
Eros so clearly betray the core of his being, his
purpose of making one out of more than one;
but when he has achieved this in the proverbial
way through the love of two human beings, he
refuses to go further.[70]

Finally, "aggressiveness forms the basis of every relation of
affection and love among people (with the single exception,
perhaps, of the mother's relation to her male child)."[71]

Freud, however, was not concerned with what is generally thought in the everyday, but rather with the knowledge which is not worthy of the name: "psychoanalysis... is
accustomed to divine secret and concealed things from un-
considered or unnoticed details, from the rubbish-heap, as it
were, of our observations."[72] He therefore placed Thanatos
not in its everyday place, and the place which it occupies in
the knowledge worthy of the name, but in its ownmost place,
the endless repetition of the primal urge which seeks to re-
gain immediately the initial inorganic state. And he placed
Eros in its ownmost place, the connecting and binding which
takes the long route to death.

What Freud says about the neurotic prohibition against
touching, in his work on taboo — and it is he who finally

abolishes taboos by the touching on them of the knowledge the absence of which they enforce as taboo precisely in order to be the taboos that they are — is suggestive here.

> The principal characteristic of the psychological constellation which becomes fixed in this way is what might be described as the subject's *ambivalent* attitude towards a single object, or rather towards one act in connection with that object. He is constantly wishing to perform this act (the touching), [and looks on it as his supreme enjoyment, but he must not perform it] and detests it as well. The conflict between these two currents cannot be promptly settled because — there is no other way of putting it — they are localized in the subject's mind in such a manner that they cannot come up against each other. The prohibition is noisily conscious, while the persistent desire to touch is unconscious and the subject knows nothing of it. If it were not for this psychological factor, an ambivalence like this could neither last so long nor lead to such consequences.
>
> In our clinical history of a case we have insisted that the imposition of the prohibition in very early childhood is the determining point; a similar importance attaches in the subsequent developments to the mechanism of repression at the same early age. As a result of the repression which has been enforced and which involves a loss of memory — an amnesia — the motives for the prohibition (which is conscious) remain unknown; and all attempts at disposing of it by intellectual processes must fail, since they cannot find any basis of attack.[73]

The translator's note to the second parenthesis in this passage explains that "From the second edition (1920) onwards, the words in square brackets were, perhaps accidentally, omitted."[74]

But, as Freud himself points out, Eros and Thanatos must be considered to have arisen together.[75] And life requires the interplay of both.[76] Furthermore, life requires the interplay of the knowledges both worthy and unworthy of the name, since these, too, arise together and presuppose each other. There are four players for every two terms in the game, and the displacements of knowledge are integral to the workings of the human organism. This is suggestive of Freud's description of marriage classes in primitive societies, given in the context of an account of the incest taboo, which prohibits illegitimate mixing in the form of a clan that touches itself too closely.[77] Now, the known prohibition appears to have reduplicated, precisely in the form of the working of the knowledge itself, the unknown prohibited action, so that what had to remain hidden, untouched even by knowledge of its precise nature, in the early history of the species, can now emerge in the later history of the individual. A zig-zag movement which is itself of some interest.

The endless repetition of broken rings is the original life which sought death; the movement of connected successive time is the death which it sought.[78] It is the latter form of the former, which is the fulfilment of the former, and which is generally called life, that Freud called death. And it is the former form of the latter, which is the unfulfilled form of the latter, which, now fulfilled, emerges for the first time, and which, generally called death, Freud called life. The emergence of the principle of constancy in the context of disorganised compulsion to repeat, instead of the other way round, as is generally thought to be the case, and as was in effect the case as long as the knowledge which was worthy of the name knew its subject to be alive.

The dead subject is, for the first time, truly alive, precisely by having died. It is alive at least in the sense that it can tolerate the recognition of itself. It is also, for the first time, truly dead. But with the invagination of the invagination which Freud inaugurated, the split of the two knowledges is complete, they can let one another be as they are, relate externally as well as internally, and there are two of the subject in each single case, completely different and completely the same, a continuity with a gap in it, or a gap with a continuity in it. Two masks, and honesty is possible by making the first mask, via the zig-zag, the same as the second. This can only be achieved by the knowledge which knows how to do as it pleases well.

The experience which is experience from the inside has nothing to do with descriptive formulations of the experience with its logic; the moment one can describe or formulate an experience one is already, in that act, outside it. This means that the moment communication occurred, and the moment the knowledge involved in communication became the determining factor in human experience, human beings were both outside and inside their own experience. Now, at the end of the life-cycle of the species, knowledge is able to catch that communicative logic, the logic of recognition, from behind, because that logic has caught the entirety of human experience from behind. The human species is therefore now completely outside its own experience, or very nearly so. And this means that, for the first time, it knows how to dispense with the determination and governance of that logic, so that, for the first time, it can be, to all practical effects and purposes, entirely inside its own experience. The individual can now relate to her/himself and to others externally as well as internally, and this internal relating can be fully so for the first time since the inception of the knowledge worthy of the name.

Proper, ownmost distinctions and differentiations, organisation which means what it says, is possible, and only upon the demise of proper, ownmost distinctions and organisation. The knowledge worthy of the name enters into its heritage, becomes knowledge worthy of the values of its life, only upon the demise of the knowledge worthy of the name. That knowledge dies, and in its death lives the individual body of knowledge, the ear and eye of which the knowledge worthy of the name always claimed to address, but from the mouth and hand of which it never really issued. Now that mouth, travelling through the inside and the outside, has caught that body from behind, and ceremonious, if scatological, exchange of gifts is possible. And with that exchange of gifts, a denial which really denies, because it knows what it does not know, and an affirmation that really affirms, because it does not know what it knows, are also possible. Freud invaginated his own invagination, and showed what it is to live well with contradiction that does not stop at contradicting the fact of itself.

After psychoanalysis comes ethics, says Lacan, ethics in the time to remember in the knowledge worthy of the name, and in the no time to forget in the knowledge not worthy of the name, may Derrida be restless in peace.

The origin Freud finds for civilisation, the murder of the father of the primal horde, belongs to the knowledge unworthy of the name; it did not necessarily occur in history. It ocurred in knowledge. It occurred as knowledge. The act of knowledge is the founding act of the human organism. The first displacement by which it registers itself in itself is the murder of origin, the presentation or presencing of absence. The lack of the lack of a lack. This significance of knowledge, presumably, is why Oedipus is identified from the start as the one who can answer the riddle of the Sphinx.

It is not inconceivable that, in historical time, the primal fathers were indeed killed by an act of knowledge, an act of recognition. The myth of Ra, whose death was brought about by the eliciting of his true name on the part of a goddess, is suggestive in this regard. It is less likely that the primal father was killed off by the sons for keeping the

167

women to himself, as Freud maintains, than that the primal fathers died as a result of the increasing familiarity with them that the women were able to gain as the community stabilised and the period of sexual availability lengthened; the males would then have been increasingly recognised — not recognised as not recognised, which would have given them the nothing required for survival — and so increasingly stimulated both by desire and by knowledge. They would have been given too much. And, as Freud points out in explaining the taboo on chieftains, "the fact that the violation of a taboo can be atoned for by a renunciation shows that renunciation lies at the basis of obedience to taboo."[79]

In this way, by a failure to renounce knowledge of them, by a failure to give nothing to them, they would have been destroyed unless they invaginated. The instant of invagination would also be the instant in which women were forgotten as the bearers of fatal knowledge. This, of course, is pure speculation. But it does have a great deal of bearing on the relation between gifts, insults, and the supersession of developmental stages.

Be that as it may, if anyone killed the effective constellation of forces in which the primal father consisted, Freud himself did, in the very act of deciding to look for such a primal origin of the social whole, a line of thought which had to invaginate and invaginate the parts whicih gave its details. It was the effects of that constellation of forces, that taken-for-granted knowledge, which ensured that the knowledge which was worthy of the name maintained its forgetfulness of the irresponsible knowledge which was not worthy of the name, the knowledge which knew too much about the workings of life and which remembered too well, and which recognised the vagina as the place which, lacking nothing, did not need to run away from where it was in order to seek, ever again, a new misrecognition, but was content to stay at home amid the uncannily stimulating bits of the forgotten social body.[80] Freud was fond of women. And he never did find out what women were wanting. And, like the primal father before him, he was right. But, unlike the primal fathers, after the completion of the life-cycle of the species, he no longer needed to give anything to get rid of his surplus, to void himself of his own waste products.

> The memory of the first great act of sacrifice thus proved indestructible, in spite of every effort to forget it; and at the very point at which men sought to be at the farthest distance from the motives that led to it, its undistorted reproduction emerged in the form of the sacrifice of the god. I need not enlarge here upon the developments of religious thought which, in the shape of rationalizations, made this recurrence possible.... "The mourning," he declares, "is not a spontaneous expression of sympathy with the divine tragedy, but obligatory and enforced by fear of supernatural anger. And a chief object of the mourners is to *disclaim responsibility for the god's death...*".[81]

Perhaps that was why Freud, the ultimate criminal, directed critical attention away from his speculative work. He, of all people, knew the significance for the organism of thought floating free from the testings of reality. But he also knew that knowledge can do as it pleases well, or it can do as it pleases badly, and he was addressing a world which did as it pleased, in the second decade of the century, extremely badly indeed.

> I hasten to add, however, that self-criticism such as this is far from binding one to any special tolerance towards dissentient opinions. It is perfectly legitimate to reject remorselessly theories which are contradicted by the very first steps

169

in the analysis of observed facts, while yet being aware at the same time that the validity of one's own theory is only a provisional one.[82]

Perhaps he had had too much of destruction to take credit for the work of realignment which his speculation signalled (perhaps as an anxiety signal), the crime against the crime of life, Hamlet's revenge consummated, the return of the name of life to what had, of overfull necessity, been given the name of death. Read *Hamlet* backwards; beginning with "Good night, sweet prince, and flights of angels sing thee to thy rest," through the death of "to sleep; perchance to dream," to the funeral, a destiny crying out, the father's ghost on the other side of death and sleep, and you have Freud, revaluer of values, hero. Can one person write both tragedy and comedy, Socrates asks at the end of his discourse on love. Freud did.

He started eating himself away with cancer of the jaw not long after the war, the death of his daughter, and *Beyond the Pleasure Principle*.[83] Not an inappropriate way of saying what he recognised in the form of failing to recognise in the times. A ceaseless repetition of reproducing cells, colonising and binding, the general form of love and life, showing its hidden succession of slow death out in the open. And the ceaseless unvarying repetition, the general form of death, hiding its compulsion of life out in the open. The man and the disease; we may assume, on the authority of Freud, that each knew as much as the other about life and death; indeed, that each was as integral a part of life and death as the other. The one a disease of the system of knowledge; the other a knowledge of the configurations of disease. The story of neither is complete without the other, and the question remains whether the disease was in the face of Freud or whether Freud was in the face of the disease.

Either way, knowledge isn't what it used to be, and neither, by the same token, are people. Nietzsche saw this before Freud; but Freud failed to see it, and failed in the right way, after Nietzsche, and that is why Freud was better at people and knowledge.

Error is cowardice, says Nietzsche, and if that is the case, then cowardice, the yielding to the pressure of one's own evaluation, is the way of the knowledge that does as it pleases well. Who, then, of Nietzsche and Freud, was the true revaluer of values? And who, then, of the two of them, acknowledged more fully and more completely the death of God?

Freud, as subtle as ever:

> If the survivors' position in relation to the dead was really what first caused primitive man to reflect, and compelled him to hand over some of his omnipotence to the spirits and to sacrifice some of his freedom of action, then these cultural products would constitute a first acknowledgement of *Ananke* (Necessity), which opposes human narcissism. Primitive man would thus be submitting to the supremacy of death with the same gesture with which he seemed to be denying it.[84]

The method of analysis allows us to repeat this error twice, making, equally, zero and four.

The four play in perpetual movement; the zero alone, the place of the error of mourning (nothing being missing in the real) and the opening which makes change and movement possible, remains constant: the enduring backside of Parmenides, in the context of the maternal invagination of which is given the play of the childish time that stands behind Heraclitus. Freud penetrated this mother of the species in the same act in which he stabbed the father of the species in the back.

IN FREUD'S DEFENCE : ECNEFeD S'DUERF NI

Let us transport ourselves into the mental life of a child. You remember the choice of object according to the anaclitic (attachment) type, which psycho-analysis talks of? The libido there follows the paths of narcissistic needs and attaches itself to the objects which ensure the satisfaction of those needs. In this way the mother, who satisfies the child's hunger, becomes its first love-object and certainly also its first protection against all the undefined dangers which threaten it in the external world — its first protection against anxiety, we may say.

In this function (of protection) the mother is soon replaced by the stronger father, who retains that position for the rest of childhood. But the child's attitude to its father is coloured by a peculiar ambivalence. The father himself constitutes a danger for the child, perhaps because of its earlier relation to its mother.... When the growing individual finds that he is destined to remain a child for ever, that he can never do without protection against strange superior powers, he lends those powers the features belonging to the figure of his father...[85]

In this act, Freud accomplished the abolition of the necessarily internal relation between Church and State, on the one hand, and the workings of the individual and the species, on the other, by the precisely inappropriate means of recognising it and so touching it in its most hidden part. He entered the holy of holies without sanction and emerged, not shining, smelling not of roses, but bearing the twin broken tablets, the remnant discarded by Moses before him, beyond the pleasure principle, on the other side of beyond, where values are made, an other side which he brought to live on this side of the dream.

Undoer of projections, in which what is internal returns from the outside, he brought the outside, which was life become death, back to its place on the inside. Everyone had remembered Narcissus, Echo, and Narcissus' reflection. Freud was the first to remember the reflection of the echo. A woman who pined away into absence through non-recognition, and who is now in a position to water with her tears (does Oscar Wilde have a place in philosophy?) the flower her ignorant object, Narcissus, became. Guilt, says Nietzsche, is an illness in the sense in which pregnancy is an illness. It became the mourning Freud delivered to the life of life.

> We may suppose, therefore, that this was the way in which things happened. The sight of a woman's dead body, naked or on the point of being stripped, reminded the young man of his mother. It roused in him a longing for his mother which sprang from his Oedipus complex, and this was immediately completed by a feeling of indignation against his father. His ideas of "father" and "God" had not yet become widely separated; so that his desire to destroy his father could become conscious as doubt in the existence of God and could seek to justify itself in the eyes of reason as indignation about the ill-treatment of a mother-object. It is of course typical for a child to regard what his father does to his mother in sexual intercourse as ill-treatment.[86]

The forward direction in which I have presented as knowledge this regressive act on Freud's part; the affirmation of the worth of pursuing, *à la* Nietzsche, the creative forward directedness of Freud's resistances, is justified by the following:

173

Nothing can be altered in the value of a cultural achievement by its being shown to have been derived from elementary animal instinctual sources.

Such a display of unfairness and lack of logic cries out for explanation. Its origin is not hard to find. Human civilization rests upon two pillars, of which one is the control of natural forces and the other the restriction of our instincts. The ruler's throne rests upon fettered slaves....

...Thus society maintains a condition of cultural hypocrisy, which is bound to be accompanied by a sense of insecurity and a necessity for guarding what is an undeniably precarious situation by forbidding criticism and discussion.... As regards the sexual instincts in the narrower sense, there is the further point that in most people they are tamed insufficiently and in a manner which is psychologlcally wrong and are therefore readier than the rest to break loose.[87]

The unexamined life is not worth living, said Socrates, who was quite something; and thereby hangs the value of a not unlikely tale.

Afterthought

These are the words of Clio, muse of history:
I was born on Mount Parnassus, a lovely
Mountain in the spring. I danced and sang
With my sisters in the ring of hyacinths
And roses on the mountain top. There, we
Often roamed abroad into the valleyed clefts
That ran in rivulets through the glistening air

We sprang in easy bounds from crag to cloud
And then again in spirals of desire
We flew to earth and nestled there
                          amid the string beans
It was often said among us that I was fair
To look upon and see. Now, however, it is wrong
To say such things. Then, it was different; the strong
Among the others felt it good and true to offer up
Such gifts to us; they were full.

They were good. We sang with them of nights
Cold and starlit, when the flames burned
And chirps watered down the blanket of silence
Fallen over the rings of flower fervour in the dark night
There was little to be said of other
Origins and such, then. We followed all
All followed and sent the youthful Hermes
To the font.

He skimmed audaciously his way and delicate
He lighted on the fountain brim, saying
Do not deny the words of Clio, muse of history.

175

Part Three

The Impotence
of Being Earnest

Introduction to Part Three

An aesthetic sensibility is a trivial thing. It requires the thoroughgoing stability of an established economic, political, cultural and social environment; otherwise it is impossible to indulge in taking such a sensibility seriously. It is, as it were, the most delicate bloom on a social formation which is already thriving strongly before aesthetic sensibility can be worth taking into account. And yet, aesthetic sensibility is also the most important thing, and the most serious thing to take into account in considering the thriving, and the strong thriving, of a society.

At the point at which the serious things, the economy, the politics, the humanly significant environment, are in crisis, those serious things are no longer there to be relied on for guidance. Under such circumstances, our guidance must come from the usually more trivial things, which do not need as urgently to be *rescued* from the crisis, since they are not very important. The most delicate bloom, as it is, in times when affairs run as a matter of course, is also, at other kinds of time, the fertilised pollen which drifts into the thriving of social necessities and the established running of affairs. It is delicate, lazy, and ethereal; it is the *by-product* of the way things are when they don't need it; but it is also the condition under which the way things are arises and has the meanings for us that it has.

As I.A. Richards said, in *The Philosophy of Rhetoric*:

> To realize that it is idle to ask of a work, "Is it beautiful?" — unless we are ready to ask thoroughly, "What will it do in its varied incidences?" — is a first step and a long step in the aesthetics of language. A parallel step must be made for every branch of aesthetics. A discussion of the reasons for the choice of words — which too often seems a trivial exchange of whimsies — can become an introduction to the theory of all choices. The art of so transforming it from a tea-table topic into the central discipline of education waits to be rediscovered, but the better we understand what place words hold in our lives the readier we shall be to admit that to think about their choice is the most convenient mode of thinking about the principle of all our choices.[1]

I suggest that political, ethical and pure theory, if there is such a thing as this last — and I do not think that it is easy to show that there isn't — cannot be properly understood without an appreciation of their relation to aesthetic sensibility. And, I suggest that the problems which arise in these kinds of enquiry cannot be solved without an appreciation of that relation, and that they *can* be solved, as far as is required at the time and in the context of the given time, given an appreciation of that relation.

What writers say, and frequently more importantly, what they do *not* say, is governed by their idea of the best form in which to present themselves and what they have to offer. This best form depends partly on the intellectual and cultural environment that they address and in which they work. When that intellectual and cultural environment changes enough, the best form in which to present these writers and what they have to offer changes as well. And what could not be said before without violating who and what was being presented and the form in which it required to be presented, if it was to *be* truly presented as what it was at the time and for the time — this *can* be said at another time and in a different context, which require, as they must, a different form of presentation.

A different emphasis of concerns appears, and the old emphasis of concerns can be resolved in ways which would have been inappropriate and untrue to the situation at the time of the old emphases. And the lessons attempted by the writers of the time may be found to be appropriately able to be given a new meaning and a differently emphasized application; and the problems that baulked them may, unaltered, be discovered to be appropriately regarded as solutions in the new context.

Images and words get their meaning from the use to which they are put both by the writer and by the reader. The point is not the image, or the word, or even the statement or argument, but what that image, word, statement or argument is used to convey. The same thing can be said in many different ways — and *must* be differently, even unrecognisably, said in different contexts with different audiences, different concerns, and different aims for which that thing is being said. And in such different contexts, the same image or way of saying something can mean or convey — and frequently *does* mean or convey — something different in each case.

Where, therefore, what is being conveyed is a logic, a way in which different things can be regarded as working together, or a process of change, or a comparison of different contexts and aims, a single image or word or statement carried all the way through that logic or process will change its meaning by degrees. At certain points it may mean *both* different things at once, or two different images, ideas or statements may carry the same meaning at the same time.

This is the same as saying that the best form in which to present something, and in which to make it truly what it is at the time and in the context, is not the same in different contexts. That form — the images, the words, the way or ways in which they are combined and ordered — is the most delicate bloom of the important thing, which is what it attempts to convey. But when one is unsure of just what that important thing is which one is trying to communicate or convey, or how best or adequately to say it, that form in which one says what one is saying, that most delicate and trivial bloom in which one at other times perhaps indulges becomes the fertilised pollen which drifts into the thriving, and the strong thriving, of the established serious and profound things that one has to say. As Oscar Wilde said, "It is only the superficial qualities that last. Man's deeper nature is soon found out."[2]

The point is still not the image, the work, the sentence or even the argument. The point is the fact that something is being said which is difficult to say. The time at which the image, word, or statement, the form of expression, is most important, is also the time when it is most futile, most trivial, most useless. But that most futile, trivial and useless activity is the condition which makes possible the effective, serious and useful presentations and communications and the meanings for us that they have.

The use of images, and the reading of images, therefore requires an aesthetic sensibility that can appreciate what it cannot or, for whatever reasons, should not say or understand at the time and in the context, and that can hold to it until enough has been presented for the context, if only subtly, to have changed. Or until the context has changed through other circumstances. And at that point, the specific images or words or arguments one uses don't matter so much any more.

Don't matter so much, except for the trivial indulgence in finding them aesthetically appreciable. Perhaps, too, all the more so in that they obscure and uselessly or pointlessly or incongruously modify what is really important in what the writer is trying to convey.

As Oscar Wilde said, "It is a very sad thing that nowadays there is so little useless information."[3]

The following tries to do justice to the triviality, uselessness and inappropriateness to which such people as Wilde committed — and still commit — their passion, their strength and their artistry.

The Impotence
of Being Earnest

> *Og*: You're castrated.
> *Earnest*: It's a woman's
> prerogative to be castrated.

In the Romantic, Symbolist or Imagist traditions, the image is that which, most detached from life in its spontaneous, natural acceptation, most contrived and unaccommodating to the tendencies of passion and useful thought, most fully embodies or enphantoms the reality of that life it abdicates and implacably repudiates. The commitment which determines and is implied by this lifelong and arduous investment in the timeless, inhuman image, on the part of so many passionate people of the last two centuries, among whom Keats, Oscar Wilde, and Yeats are exemplary, as, in a clumsier, more brutal way, are Marx and Freud, with the strange commitment of the first, brilliant and lucid as he was, to the stupidity of matter and of lumpish masses, and the rhetorically ingenious and perverse commitment of the second, prudishly severe and scientifically rigorous as he was, to the erect penis, than which nothing is more detached from human intelligence and the spontaneous tendencies of human passions, which it attempts to end as rapidly as possible: the commitment which determines and is implied by this lifelong and arduous investment in the timeless, inhuman image, on the part of so many passionate people, is a commitment to making the best of life, to life or reality as it is most beautiful.

This is the commitment of sensibility or taste, in an irredeemably ugly and nauseating world, a world which perpetually destroys what there is to be appreciated by treating it as secondary, ultimately relegating it to phantasy, literature and, most grossly, to social irresponsibility. You should, the grossest say, do your part, put your part in, as it were, into the social or common good: and don't say that the common good is so common that it barely merits the dignity of being considered uncommonly bad; there's nothing to be appreciated but what *we* appreciate, and if you say differently we'll *make* you listen, because we appreciate so much what there is to be appreciated.

Now, people of sensibility know that one can't *force* people to appreciate, to be deeply moved with delight, and that as soon as one is in a context constituted first and foremost by relations of power, then the beautiful, that which is to be appreciated purely for the fact of its existence, cannot be engaged with that context. In a *world* like that, sensibility or taste must and can only commit itself to a completely different realm, to splitting off reality, the world a minimally decent god or minimally decent people *might* have made, splitting it off completely from the mundane, which is left to be contemptible and without any longer being thinkable, even *thinkable*, as something which can be made the best of, to which real value, value to which one might find it worth committing oneself and making sacrifices for — to which, in short, real beauty and real delight are not thinkable as notions that apply except in the form of wishes, sighs, bitterness, and, worst, resignation.

Thus Plato's method returns, but this time for the opposite reasons, not, as before, to gain control over the events and activities of the mundane world, but now, these mundane events and activities being thoroughly controlled with the worst effects on the possibilities of human life and reality, to escape this control, to escape the mundane world which had lost the sense of why it was controlling in the first place.

The world had made use of a method given its meaning by a commitment to making the best of sense to make the best of things, and now was pervasively committed to the method, the control, blindly and stupidly, to the exclusion of the aspirations which alone give method, control and knowledge their meaning, and establishing — pervasively and actively — the exclusion of those aspirations by that unthinking commitment itself. Formerly, method, ways of doing things, as a whole, could be questioned, and justification could therefore be provided and tested. Now, questioning and reasoned justification were exercised everywhere for their own sake, without themselves any longer being subject to question, and therefore without themselves being capable any longer of justification. The method or way of making the best of sense to make the best of things was now itself as a whole being used in the worst of ways, without questioned and reasoned method, and in all areas of life, which thereby lost their individual specificity and with that their specific identity with what *did* belong in the same area. Gross universalisation and crass disappearance of specific commonality.

Consequently nothing *could* make sense any more, unless blind stupidity is taken to be the highest achievement conceivable in human reality; and the only option for those still unfortunately ravaged by a commitment to a liveable life, a life in which intelligence, taste and passion could play a committed part, the only option was insanity in the terms of the mundane world, in accordance with the dominating reality, and a truly sane commitment to beauty and reality as the hopeless and unattainable, still in accordance with the truth of the dominant reality.

Sensibility, in short, is that which tells one when things are not as they should be: it interposes a sheet of nausea between what one is involved in or what one is doing and the way things *should* be if one were able to do or be differently.

187

This can apply to a situation one is in, in which case everything would have to change by a miraculous process of turning inside out or leaping to something completely different in some other way, before one could act in accordance with the reality as it is *and* act simply in accordance with the unqualified delight of one's sensibility; or it can apply to oneself in relation to oneself, in which case the same change or kind of change is the only way out.

Sensibility is also the root of pure unqualified delight, of wholehearted passionate and joyous engagement in the life which yields to and affirms sensibility, of good conscience in a world in which good conscience is appropriate, is true to the reality of that world.

It is one's sense of *the fact that*, or *the fact of*, something's being what it is, as the whole of what it is, including what it can be, in the way in which it is that. It is the knowledge one has of something before one knows it, and which is the first step of the knowledge one may come to have, orienting one for that knowledge in the way suited to the fact that one is what oneself is. It is objective: it says truly what one is in relation to that something, and consequently is the condition for objective knowledge of the something, as that something truly is for who one truly is. It is the sense of what is fitting for a thing given the fact of what that thing is, and therefore allows one to know what details belong to that thing in what order of significance, so that it is possible to come to know the thing in *its* details, and not merely in the confusion of its details with those of its particular contexts.

Sensibility itself, the root of good conscience, determines one to act in accordance both with the mundane reality *and* the way it should be if it were best, since sensibility is very much continuous, very strongly of the substance of, both the world as it *is* and the world as it *can* be. It is truly committed, yearns in *fact* for, the best that can be made of things, and consequently sees objectively, as no other motivation can, the world as it is, irrespective of the cost (extreme torment doesn't come from nowhere, nor is it experienced without an extreme willingness to become engaged in the reality of that which causes it. It is possible simply not to be aware at any level, as is the case, for example, with most people, who are not truly committed to their yearnings). Sensibility or taste *must* see or respond objectively, because that is the only way it can make its world better, or thoroughly better, or completely different.

If the world is such that the notions of beauty, delight and values of fulfilment have no place in it, if that is its reality, then sensibility will act in accordance with that reality, will abandon that world, split itself in two, and find its fulfilment in a realm it creates to be completely detached from the now mundane world. It will commit itself permanently to a life of nausea, and celebrate that as the ideal for life as it is lived, or take a permanent revenge on that life, in itself and in its surroundings, in either case committing itself to isolation to and beyond the point of madness, while it finds a pure beauty in the image that has no connection, no engagement, nothing to do or to be done, with anything.

Such was the world of the Romantics. But things have changed, and now the same commitment to making things and life beautiful, making it the kind of life and world yielding to and engaging in whole-hearted joyous and passionate engagement, pure and unqualified delight, full and untrammelled thinking, passion, imagining, yearning and doing, in the context of, fed and nurtured and anchored by, the full power of unashamed, unriven, uncomplicated sensibility and taste; this commitment is now best served precisely by the opposite method or approach.

Now the world can — or at least there is a good chance, and that is all unsatisfied yearning needs — yield or be put in a position to yield to the engagements of sensibility. Of course appreciation of what is appreciable for taste cannot itself be forced on the context, since that betrays the very principle of taste, as it really is, itself; but the world is now such that the resistances to seeing and appreciating what there is to be seen and appreciated can frequently be bent back on themselves, purely with their co-operation — that is, spontaneously co-operate in recognising themselves as resistances, making them, for the first time, resistances or attitudes and knowledge of those attitudes, for *both* points of view, instead of being these for the one and meaningless impulsive forces for the other — so that those who still retain some vestiges of sensibility or even its full complement can stumble, in time, on what could not be forced on them — on what it is that their resistances are resisting, so that these things become, for the first time, things which are given for *both* points of view, instead of being given to the one and empty talk for the other — and decide in what direction they wish to follow their yearnings, towards engagement in the world of delights and concomitant sacrifices, or towards passivity or gloomy and mysterious forebodings of a world to come or vanish.

It is time for the Romantic to become scientist and logician, in order to travel to the very centre of the nausea of things and a world and life gone wrong, basically wrong before one started, always already wrong, and there to turn inside out.

And it is time for the Romantic to become warrior and strategist, rhetorician and tactician, howling wolf and shadowing eagle, contemptible dribbling moron and savage monstrous madman, God and priest and celibate and leper, saint and magician and odious refuse, hero and coward and turd and poison, in order to fight against those still outside in who would prevent the return of even the minimally decent, or rather of the tremendous delicious context in which such minimal decency could find its root and its only ultimate reality, the context of a commitment and a set of practices which make real that commitment in a world which yields to and affirms, if only sometimes and in spots, the lubricious magnificence of that wholehearted delight, that piercing, full and unhindered simplicity of truly loving, festively engaged, sensibility.

Incredibly beautiful things can happen, and can be made to happen; first sensibility must betray itself as never before; and then sensibility must insist on itself, as never before.

First sensibility must betray itself by committing itself to the ugliest, to the world of which it is a part, the contemporary world; it must look up its own asshole, analyse itself, dissect itself, spread itself out shamelessly and in the most vulgar way, removing whatever is left to it of subtlety, of its own most proper life of irony, dissimulation, guise, and the making of spaces for human life that is the *raison d'être* of that subtlety, of what it, sensibility, is itself.

Then it must find in that shamelessly betrayed vulgarity, displayed and spread out, a new sensibility, a completely new way of making sense, of engaging with the world, of making beautiful and making the best of things, a beauty and a best and a language of practices and images which have never existed before.

This is possible, and therefore necessary for those so inclined, because the contemporary world is one which has never existed before, precisely in the way that it excludes all possibility of real engagement so as to make a difference, all possibility of satisfying sensibility and idiosyncratic yearning.

The Romantics could do it through art, through the detached image itself. The image has now become incorporated into the mundane, however, to the degree that the mundane is itself detached from all life that yearns, that desires, all human life.

The mundane has become the realm of the timeless, inhuman image, self-begotten, indifferent to human passions and concerns, a gigantic cynical re-run of all that was ever taken seriously, for no purpose or end other than the fact of its own existence, less cynical than mocking of all purely human endeavours and experiences, less mocking than accidentally affecting its spare parts, human beings and human desires, as it pursues its indifferent, cosmic path.

This makes reality such that we can ourselves understand how to treat things as really just simply there, for no other purpose than the fact of their own existence: and that includes our own desires. We don't need, to justify our existence and give us a purpose, God or gods anymore, nor a justification and purpose which is given by a society or community; we can rest on our own desires, our own purposes, as simply there. But, unlike what the divine or social images have become, our desires are the kind of image with which we can do something, with which we can engage ourselves in the world; our desires are brute facts which, nonetheless, we can get inside of; they are *living* facts, and they are *our* life.

And that is why it is now possible to find a new beauty, a new best of things, a new sensibility, to commit oneself to. Social reality no longer requires that we take it seriously; in fact it requires the reverse, since it no longer takes itself seriously. Furthermore, social reality has made itself, which includes us, such that anything is as valuable, ultimately, as anything else, anything can go for a high price given the right circumstances, and be worth fighting over, so that each individual, each idiosyncratic desire, is as valuable, ultimately, as anything else. The reality that sensibility has to take into account therefore includes this possibility, that it doesn't have to take anything into account except what it wants; and that possibility is all it needs, since the fact that it is *social* reality which makes this true, means that sensibility can now be responsibly and intelligently committed, fully engaged in its context and the world, *by* taking into account only what it wants.

The problem is now solely whether anything good can be made by sensibility of what it wants in conjunction with what other people independently want.

The answer to that question requires that we look, as sensibility has always required, very closely at what it is that we want, and that includes, for people of sensibility, people who yearn for something better, and are nauseated by what is not right in the way things are, when it is not right, that we look very closely at sensibility itself.

In this way sensibility overcomes itself, turns inside out through itself, or leaps to somewhere completely different.

This cannot be accomplished by force, because appreciation, which is what sensibility is all about, does not live in the same locus as force. This is evident from, and explains, the fact that sensibility is perpetually nauseated in or absent from the contemporary world, which knows only force and constraint and what is useful, effective — in short, forceful or powerful.

The idealistic and earnest are impotent, all idiosyncratic desire and all yearning is impotent, in this world. Impotence, castration, are significant terms to us, the end of the world, precisely because power is so highly valued. If we can regard impotence or castration as irrelevant, and only if we can do that, can we escape the determinations, the markings, the inscriptions on our bodies of power and power relations, and allow — not force — allow the free and spontaneous resurgence of the joy of intense sensibility, of intense appreciation, and of action, thought and feeling on the basis of that affirming, yes-saying appreciation.

Sensibility and its reality have a potency of their own: not by any means a potency to dominate, to insist, to enslave, or to abandon responsibility and be enslaved, to the detriment of those then given the responsibility in an unsupporting world; on the contrary, a potency to accept and discriminate the individuality of experience and experiences, an immense flooding of joy, of delight, of disappointment, of horror, of terror, of shock, of anger, of serenity, of enduring appreciation: and, more important, a quiet and subtle sense of enjoyment, of dislike, of definitive discrimination, and of the value of small differences and changes.

Sensibility is alien to power because it would not disturb a hair of that which it appreciates; and it would not stop that which it appreciates from changing in the ways it chooses.

Sensibility is the affirmation which is the floor of the world, which says, yes, this is real and I would sustain it as such, and which, with saying that affirms, as Nietzsche insists, everything connected with that reality, and that everything is, indeed, everything there is. Once that affirmation has taken place, power and disapproval and approval and active selection and organisation are free to return as far as sensibility is concerned, but without sensibility they are not in the locus in which appreciation exists fully as what it is. Sensibility gives everything else its meaning and its worth, as far as human beings and human desire is concerned.

In the light of which considerations, it may be worth considering whether the entirety of human history and of cultures up until now (to borrow the phrase of encouragement "up until now" from Foucault) have not, because of the emphasis on power and force, prevented the appearance of what there is in human terms to be appreciated, and whether much of history cannot be appreciated for what it is without considering the machinations of a hidden sensibility which could only, slowly, patiently and tirelessly, bend back on themselves the resistances against appreciating what there is to be appreciated, until people were in a position to stumble, unforced, on these realities. Contemporary society would then be the ultimate resistance of a world governed by a power/impotence opposition to the humiliation of finding out that it never knew what was going on. Of course, that would not be a humiliation if knowledge wasn't lived as a form of power; but if knowledge wasn't subordinated, like everything else, ultimately, to the opposition of power/impotence, sensibility would already have had full play, and the objectivity required by a realistic wish to make things better would have been the norm long ago, so that people would have known what was going on. The pieces are either fundamentally all in the right places for a form of life or thought or appreciation, or they're fundamentally in the wrong places.

It is also worth considering the possibility that this historical process was necessary in order that individuals be able to handle such appreciation without the support of an institutionally organised community. Or, alternatively, that sensibility and what is there to be appreciated created themselves gradually through the workings of power, and vice-versa. Or, as yet another alternative, that the question of history is a purely aesthetic matter, for more-or-less profound satisfaction and enjoyment, not for rigorous knowledge.

In any event, the point is that history is the history of the present, and where the present has more than one meaning, for more than one point of view, there is more than one history. The important feature of the history of such a present is the way in which *that* history succeeds in the present in being a simultaneity of independent histories, at once both one and many.

Thirdly, then, sensibility must insist on itself as never before, in its new form and substance, using the old form and substance as its guise, dissimulation and protective surface against the power/impotence axiom that blindly, and being blind, ruthlessly, opposes it. It can keep destroying itself in the form and substance it formerly constituted or had, because the spaces for human life, desire and possibility which it is its business to create, sustain and nurture are now embodied in a new form and substance; they are new spaces, new human realities, which are invisible to the eye of power, not affected by it except insofar as they are not permitted to exist, to be inhabited or explored, at all. If it is possible for the pieces to be in the right places for a form of life, thought, or appreciation, then the pieces belonging to another form of life, thought or appreciation are, from that point of view, simply in the wrong places, and that's that.

But one must be committed to the fact that impotence, castration, humiliation are completely, completely irrelevant, and be prepared to engage in activities that make one look like a worm, a freak, a hopeless schizo, without either expecting or, at bottom, desiring, that one should appear differently, unless the spectator or spectators are prepared of their own desire to see what is there to be appreciated, in which case they undergo the same humiliation, *they* become the worms, the freaks, the contemptible morons and incompetents: their judgment turns on themselves.

In terms of the old order, they atone for their misdeeds and/or you get your revenge; in terms of the new order, your reality is affirmed, they can live in a world in which tremendous appreciation is really appropriate and possible to act on the basis of, a world to which they can say, yes, with glee; and you may both have gained really good friends with whom you can share your passions and who can support you without judgment when you need such support.

The path is incredibly hard, even unthinkably hard, but the rewards are such as to consume one with unmitigated, raging, and enduring fury that it should have been necessary to go through such nightmare to get to what alone can found even a minimally decent world; and to fill one with intense gratitude that even minimal decency is possible despite the occasional nightmare quality of things.

The way in which things have changed in relation to the Romantic approach or method is identifiable in very concrete ways.

The Romantics, in order to make the best of things, to make life as beautiful, as appropriate for joy, as possible, invested themselves in the image as detached from everyday life as possible. Now everyday life has become as detached from all life, life in general, including everyday life, as possible. No one sees or knows what they're doing, and if you point it out unmistakeably to them they become bewildered: they don't know what to do with living realities and living things, and they can't bear to see how unliving they are. Furthermore, it is in fact possible to make life beautiful, to appreciate beautiful and bizarre things in it, precisely *because of* this change: the beautiful Romantic image *is*, now, everyday life. Consequently, the way to carry out the mission of Romantic sensibility, to make life as beautiful, as appreciable as it can be, is to engage in it most fully as everyday, mundane life, in accordance with one's everyday, mundane, desires. That everyday, mundane life then acquires the tones and textures and splendours, the aloof, untouchable beauty, capable of and demanding reverence and exultation and contemplative satisfaction, aimed at and achieved by the Romantics in the form of the image.

But many other things have changed as well, and to make this one apparently simple change, one has to undergo a circuit through all the connected parts of the reality that has changed. And in our homogenised, technique-ridden and knowledge-pervaded world everything is connected to everything else, so that *everything* has to change, bit by bit, each with its threefold movement followed by a pirouette as one goes on to the next, until enough bits have been gone through to suck the rest along with them, when one can make the final pirouette, have a cup of tea without bothering to work anything out any more, in a world one can be satisfied with, with plenty of possibilities, and company which has the eyes to see without judging, objectively, before it chooses to judge.

Of course, it is precisely *because* everything is connected to everything else that everything has to change for anything worth changing to change; but it is also because everything is connected that it is *possible* to change everything, and for those who want to live in a world in which power can be irrelevant, that is a very good thing.

One of the key points of change is that of the meaning of power and humiliation, because these are key axioms of the world which needs to be changed, and of which we are part as we attempt to change. What was or is taken to be powerful victory and triumph, needs to be understood as humiliating stupidity, the most shameful thing to do or feel. What used to be extreme humiliation needs to be understood as powerful triumph and victory.

In terms of sensibility, appreciating what is there to be appreciated, this simply *is* so. Macho strutting, as a form of power rather than decorative display, is the most absurdly ridiculous thing in a world in which no one is in control and everybody is terrified of their most intimate desires. It's simply a cowardly lie. Total self-abnegation, on the other hand, allowing someone to trample victoriously over your raped and terrified spirit, is a devastating vengeance, a terribly humiliating blow, because it shows the other person up for what they are, in the eyes of sensibility, that which is not too terrified to say yes to life in all its forms, that is, to acknowledge the *existence* of what is there, in unqualified terror or dislike or joy, all of which presuppose that acknowledgement without reservation.

Of course, once the world of sensibility is available for mutual inspection, the one who was humiliated by being victorious is now the victorious one, since s/he was humiliated, and the one who was victorious by being humiliated is now the humiliated one, since s/he was victorious.

But the pieces now function in a different way, for different purposes and with different meanings.

In the world of sensibility, humiliation and victory over people are not ends in themselves or the end of the world, they are only necessary because people cannot appreciate what is there to be appreciated. As soon as people can do so, the humiliation and victory are matters of a purpose which no longer applies, is more or less trivial.

In any event, both parties are now both victor and victim, loser and winner, hero and coward, when both worlds are considered together.

This displays the same logic as the reversal of the Romantic position, a reversal which is the only way to maintain its own intention and aim. There, the most artificial was formerly the most alive; now the alive is most artificial: therefore the alive is most alive but in a completely new sense and experience of what life is, in which artificial and natural are not only distinguished as opposed on the same evaluative scale, or scale of values, but are also different ways of doing the same thing, and in fact different ways of being each other. Here, the cowardly was formerly the most heroic (the Romantic hero, not committed to anything "realistic," "running away from the harsh realities of life"); now the heroic is the most cowardly: therefore the heroic is most heroic, but in a completely new sense of heroism, in which heroism and cowardice are not only distinguished as opposed on the same scale of values or evaluative scale, but are also different ways of doing the same thing, and in fact different ways of being each other.

All opposed values work in this way, when two fundamentally incompatible understandings are both at issue, and sensibility itself does too, except that it is opposed to itself. Each opposite is both opposite to and, independently of this, *is* the other with a different and opposed emphasis, the other upside down, the other with an opposed priority, since the same actions and feelings and thoughts, the same pieces of reality, are conceivable under the commitments to either of the opposed values, but co-ordinated differently, with a different rhythm or scansion, different kinds of effects in the long and short term, and so on. Each discloses or reveals a world to be seen in a certain way.

Sensibility affirms all worlds as existing and as having a point of view; it may or may not wish to participate in certain worlds, but it does not condemn or approve of them except as a matter of its own preference or purposes, *never* as a matter of truth. To say that something simply *is* something else, without specifying a point of view and a commitment and a purpose, outside of any of which what the something is is up for grabs, doesn't even begin to make sense. It is literally meaningless, except as a verbal object at which one can only gawk, or hang on one's wall as a conversation piece.

The gaining of objective knowledge is of course a purpose for which one can say that something is something. But it is, nonetheless, a *particular* purpose in the peculiar sense of presupposing a particular form of life, language and commitments. The objective knowledge is universal, *for that particular* form of life. This is, on the one hand, the least significant way in which a purpose can be particular, can be meaningfully called a purpose at all, since universality and particularity are given their meanings only *within* an *already* presupposed form of life. It is, on the other hand, the most significant way in which a purpose can be particular, since its recognition allows the new recognition of other forms of life, and the appreciation of one's own form of life as a whole, such as is found in philosophy and art.

Such recognition and appreciation is the work of sensibility, which is at the boundaries of objective knowledge and at its heart. It is the same sense which allows one to know, for example, when one has used the same word too many times. And to do its work, it needs to be kept in working order, which requires a certain kind of discipline in one's life, internal and external, a discipline rooted in an objective knowledge of sensibility itself.

Another key point of change, especially pertinent to people already possessed to a large degree of active sensibility, is that of naivety and sophistication, innocent blatantness and decadent, cultivated worldliness.

What is taken to be worldly sophistication is in fact blatantly and blindly naive, in that it is unable to relax into what is there to be appreciated, let alone acknowledge its existence as what it is in its own right. It is a form of domination and power abuse, with impoverishing effects. Innocence or naivety is tremendously receptive and aware, firmly based on reality, which is why children can be so objective and discerning. Naivety, or what is taken to be naivety, is in fact the root of sensibility itself.

However, in a complicated and hideously disfiguring and lying world, naivety has to learn to protect itself, and, being trusting in the sense that it takes for granted that other realities do exist and in their own right, it learns to lie and not know it when it is told by everyone and everything that lies are truth.

Fortunately, nausea exists as a recourse for sensibility to let itself know, as do shame and bad conscience.

Consequently innocence comes to commit itself, with all its affirming strength and desperate refusal to acknowledge unreality and nay-saying, to sophistication. But sophistication is blind and cannot see the lies, nor how trivial a thing it is to abandon them. What needs to happen is that sophistication come to see itself as naive, and naivety come to see itself as truly sophisticated and aware of the world, in order that naivety can stop holding on to blind sophistication and so blocking its perceptions. and sophistication can stop hampering itself with the seriousness of innocence, which knows too much.

It is sophistication and cultivated decadence that are truly innocent, truly unknowing of what they do at a fundamental level, that are truly playful. And while naive awareness may not know the rules of the particular game that is being played, it certainly always knows what's at stake.

Innocence, that is, is aware of the significance of the *fact that* the game is being played. While the artificiality of sophistication, in order to be artificial, has to overlook the spontaneity shown in the *fact of* the *aspiration to be* artificial, of the *possibility of* that aspiration, and of the possibility of its achievement. And the spontaneous overflow of powerful feelings, on the other hand, is born amid the urine and feces of bloodless abstraction — the categories, concepts, logics and purely artificial unprecedented departures that initiate the establishment of such abstractions in the world — which allow those feelings to be experienced as what they are, and not something else; and which emerge in the fact of the expression of those spontaneities as the specific spontaneities they are.

Innocence is the finished product of a taken-for-granted process of cultivation and sophistication; the process of cultivation is the finished product of a taken-for-granted innocence. This is, of course, only true when and as long as it's a matter of making room for more than one, or for the possibility of more than one, disparate sensibility. But on such occasions, this is *strictly* true.

In order to be present in accord with the sensibility in which it consists, naivety should be hidden behind sophisticated decadence, using it as its guise and dissimulation, in such a way that it can be guessed at and enjoyed by other hidden naiveties, except perhaps at times of intimacy.

And in order to be present in accord with the innocence in which it consists, decadent worldly cultivation should play freely in the public space, in the context of the innocence which is there to know whether and when it matters what's at stake, when seriousness, maturity, is required.

This development engages with the issue of humiliation: sophistication is regarded as a form of power, of status.

Again, the humiliation must be undergone, in order to discover that one is in fact sophisticated, deeply knowing of culture, precisely in allowing oneself to be humiliated, that one is innocent precisely in the degree to which one felt decadent, used up, bored, and having seen it all; and that not only does it not matter, but that it is *appropriate* to be innocently cultivated and decadent, and to be naive with the innocence of sensibility.

And now, too, one *knows* what's what; everything has changed, and nothing has changed, and one is in a completely revaluated world in which for the first time it's possible to *know* what's going on as far as one needs to, and what one needs to know is not very much, unless one enjoys knowledge, in which case the more the better.

One uproots the tree of sensibility, destroys it by turning it sideways and showing its roots — that is, one gradually confirms and establishes it in knowledge, in the accepting recognition of the fact that it is what it is — which turn out to be very well adapted to knowing what's going on out in the open, so that one discovers, aghast, that it was the branches and leaves which were easily misled, and which are more comfortable underground; so that it turns out to be a very good thing that sensibility destroyed itself that way, since it was upside down to begin with, and can now be replanted, but the same way up as before, because one is in a position now to see that the earth and the air were also upside down before, so that the tree was in fact correctly planted. The difference is that now one knows clearly and in a way which one can now consciously appreciate, enjoy, and cultivate in the way of its diverse fruits, what one knew only vaguely, wishfully, incompletely, uncertainly, at great risk, before. Now the risks are simply risks, because now one is operating fully and simply in accord with the roots of one's sensibility, which knows that nothing is at stake *except what one* wants to make of things, and fully and simply in accord with one's cultivated decadence, which knows that a great deal can be made, as long as one is able and prepared to act on what one wants.

In short, the limp penis, the penis only slowly waking to arousal, is seriously underestimated. The unresistant, uninsistent weight of such a penis is a wonderful thing in which to indulge.

What one needs, I think, if one desires to make the most of life, is a capacity for a spontaneous and committed limpness at the times and in the places at which negotiation between different styles and priorities of life is the pressing requirement.

The erect manhood of Marx's proletariat, proud to overcome; the rigid urgency of a Nietzsche; the competent penetration of a Freud, delaying the gratification of conclusion until the subject matter is ready to come to voice: all these have their place, their importance, and their distinguishable degrees and kinds of instructive and admirable achievement, of political, aesthetic and spiritual significance.

They are not *opposed* to the limpidity of the limp wrist, the half-aroused eye, the dangling action, however. They *presuppose* it, *as* their opposite, *as* that with which they are incompatible. It is the context within which they occur if they occur meaningfully. Without this limpness to fall back on, they are just shots in the dark, and worthwhile only as shots in the dark.

Politics which has learned from Marx, either by further development or by rejection; aesthetics which has learned from Nietzsche how to give an account of tastes, evaluations and lifestyles, whether comparable to his particular account or disparate with it; thinkings and therapies which have learned from Freud how or how not to develop a framework within which to deal with human experience: all these must understand — if they are to understand themselves and how to achieve their ends without defeating those ends in the very act of going about trying to accomplish them — that what Keats called the negative capability of not knowing, the capacity to be actively unable to insist, is that without which fundamental change, and the mutual making of space for the flourishing of individual and social differences, cannot be.

Whoever wants to live in a non-oppressive world, and to make for the possibility of such a world, in their own environments or more generally, must learn, in their own way, the beauty and the satisfactory experience of something like the limp penis. Such a person must learn to let events arise of their own accord, in their own way, because otherwise one is simply repeating the acts of violence in which oppression consists.

The point of this book has been that there *is* such a thing as letting things arise of their own accord and in their own way. So far, as I understand it, that realisation has been confined within the terms of understandings that, taken as a whole, are oppressive in our own day. The difficulty is to articulate that realisation with the terms of understandings which are not, in our own day, oppressive, and that is difficult because these understandings have, as I understand it, restricted themselves to taking the traditional accounts or views exclusively as wholes, or as a whole.

In other words, we need to be able to do two things, if we are to be able to think in a non-oppressive way of things as arising of their own accord. The first is to be able to recognise that and how the same parts can be completely different in two or more completely different wholes. The second is to be able to recognise that and how two or more completely different wholes can be identical with respect to the same parts.

We must therefore be able to recognise parts as the same even while they are in fact completely different, being given their meaning by being parts in two or more completely different wholes. And we must, therefore, be able also to recognise as wholes, entire unto themselves, what are in fact parts, being considered in relation to parts which exist as what they are in relation also to other wholes. And vice-versa, since these wholes which are parts of a situation including other such wholes are each identifiable on their own account.

The only way to do all this is simply to let, from the start, the two or more wholes be together, in whatever way they are in each case. And this means letting things arise, from the start, of their own accord and in their own way.

In other words, we have to assume the solution of the difficulty before we start trying to solve it.

This means, in terms of pure theory, the following.

We're not in a position to know whether the difficulty,

when we're dealing with a whole understanding, can be solved or not. The only way to solve it is to assume that it's already solved, and then go ahead and find what one has assumed.

This is circular: but that's not the point.

The point is that one makes a decision either way: one takes the risk that it can be solved, and by doing so ensures that it will be; or one takes the risk that it can't be solved, and by doing so ensures that it will not be. *Either* way is circular.

But by finding which circle one finds oneself having entered, or which risk one finds oneself having taken, one has let things arise of their own accord, and in their own way. *That* is not circular.

And decisions based on that are not oppressive — they do not impose one's circular self-justifications on people and circumstances. And they are not relative and arbitrary — they are simply honest: and since one is also oneself part of the reality of the circumstances one is in, they are, by being honest, based on the simple truth of the situation.

It is the logic of this kind of knowledge that this book attempts to articulate, in the contexts both of fundamental change over time and of the simultaneity of fundamentally different understandings.

And this logic, in each context in which I have dealt with it, involves the necessity, at some point or for some period, of limpness, in which, as it were, the substance of what is happening needs to be both fully and loosely fitted with what keeps it in its shape, to be loosely held so as to be able to be pulled either way, in which its skin is not too tightly stretched by the demands of the substance to allow anything but one conclusion.

This point of firm limpness can of course be maintained in its own right, but the point here is that a definite absence or definite insistence of further engagement or commitment presupposes, if it is to be true both to desire and to honesty—if it is to be true—at least a point of such limpness.

I have identified that point, in general terms, above, in talking about finding the decision, the risk, one has already made or taken. The way in which one establishes the possibility of doing that is by cultivating that feel of the limp weight of the issue, unresistant and uninsistent, and gently exploring the long and the short of it.

It is this that those who have learnt from Marx, Nietzsche and Freud, I think, need to understand: the only way to have arrived responsibly in a position to accept or reject *any* understanding, is to have come via that point or period of limpness.

It is that point the significance of which I have attempted to establish and articulate, in politics, ethics, aesthetics and pure theory. I have tried to show, given knowledge understood as a form of power (by categorisation of people, for example), that by taking this understanding to its extreme one emerges correctly, truthfully, at the opposite understanding. Given the human individual understood as a collection of drives, this understanding taken to its extreme emerges at the opposite understanding. Given Romanticism, this understanding taken to its extreme emerges at Realism and Classicism: the fitting place for the fitting thing at the fitting time.

And the overriding point of all this is that we can think these incompatible opposites together, and not, in so doing, removing their incompatibility, but in fact *only by* maintaining that incompatibility. Conversely, their incompatibility is truly maintained only by, at some point, allowing them to be thought together.

It is their complete incompatibility, their complete mutual support, their complete indifference and absence of relation, incompatible or otherwise, that I wanted to show how to think in one kind of thought, and the significance of that thinking for each of these things, thought separately.

This is all, of course, as practical as it is theoretical;

and for that kind of thought and practice, as what Marx calls a sensuous practical activity, I cannot think of a better place to start, along with many others, than the satisfactory experience of the limp penis, and the difference the cultivation of that experience may make to what, completely different, and to be thought of entirely in its own terms, precedes it, and to what, completely different, and to be thought of entirely in its own terms, may follow it.

As Plato has Socrates say of lovers in the *Phaedrus:*

> And so, if the victory be won by the higher elements of mind guiding them into the ordered rule of the philosophical life, their days on earth will be blessed with happiness and concord, for the power of evil in the soul has been subjected, and the power of goodness liberated; they have won self-mastery and inward peace.
>
> ...He who is not a lover can offer a mere acquaintance flavored with wordly wisdom, dispensing a niggardly measure of worldly goods; in the soul to which he is attached he will engender an ignoble quality extolled by the multitude as virtue, and condemn it to float... bereft of understanding.
>
> Thus, then, dear god of love ... grant me thy pardon for what went before, and thy favor for what ensued; be merciful and gracious, and take not from me the lover's talent wherewith thou hast blessed me; neither let it wither by reason of thy displeasure, but grant me still to increase in the esteem of the fair.... Then will his disciple here present no longer halt between two opinions, as now he does, but live for Love in singleness of purpose with the aid of philosophical discourse.[1]

I suggest, then, that the hope of fundamental change from one whole way of living to another which Marx located in the revolution of the working classes, Nietzsche in the entire revaluation of values, and Freud in the thorough working through of unconscious resistances, is truly to be measured by the weight and practice of firm limpness, the force of which lies in making spaces for things to arise of their own accord, and in their own way.

Revolution, new evaluation and recognition, understood in terms of what they aim at, which gives them their meaning, rather than in terms of what they come from, which denies them their meaning, are in themselves irrelevant. Their meaning germinates in the dampness of a moist welcome to exploration; if the exploration has the meaning of revolution, new evaluation, or new recognition, it will want, eagerly, to be tentative, to do justice to what it is coming to love.

If the exploration does not want this, then it simply does not have the meaning of revolution, new evaluation, or new recognition; it denies that meaning, iis not concerned with doing justice, or with love, honesty and truth, but exclusively with self-glorification, without intelligence or discrimination, with trying to prove the superior length to which it will go, or the superior size of its membership, in a vain effort to compensate, by diminishing everything else, for the inadequacy of the only member which has any significance for it.

The fires of revolution and liberatory change, then, are there to make space for the relish of a damp morning in Spring. Marx said that the principle of the social formation established by revolution must, if the revolution is to establish the kind of community it aims at and not some other, be the principle of the revolution itself, since the act of revolution is the establishment of the principle of that community. The principle of these passions and fires, then, must be wet.

And what comes after that, comes freely, and possibly with love.

To Keats

Once upon a summer clipped a
Philosopher a rainbow's wings and
Lo! The rainbow smiled and droplets
Each a thousand rainbows wild and
Scintillating free within the fragments
Of his burst asunder words and peri
Phrases left a logic burning with
Desire and the tropes of many
Mysteries kept unassuaged to
Journey in the prepositions of
A proposition glimpsed through smiling
Laughter and the tears of a not yet
There when once upon a twice how
Many numbers smoothly flowing yet
They pause what to but to reflect
Reflect I say the flashing gleam of
That achieved but not yet there and
So complete in this that when the
Words are beckoning me O letter
Writer what beyond is here when
All the words have given is a
B and c and nothing captured
But the glimpse beyond futurity
Whose now — the glimpse's — is
This other side the rainbow yes
O friend my yearning leaves the
Page and here beyond the yet

Of that futurity its not
Its here the bluebirds fly on
This side of the page and Vera
Lynn unsullied sings left free
To not a nightingale but a
Phrase which captured sings the
Melody of all the ways the words
Did love not what they touched not
On.

Notes

Introduction to Part One

[1] Shaw, G.B., *Man and Superman: A Comedy and a Philosophy.* Harmondsworth: Penguin Books Ltd., 1957, "Epistle Dedicatory," p. 32.

[2] Wilde, O., *Complete Works of Oscar Wilde.* (Vyvyan Holland, Ed.) London: Collins, 1966. "Phrases and Philosophies for the Use of the Young," p. 1206.

[3] Shaw, G.B., *Ibid.,* p. 34.

[4] Boston: Beacon Press, 1987.

Part One: Eulogy: How To Speak Well

[1] More, T., *Utopia,* Paul Turner, trans., (Harmondsworth: Penguin Books Ltd., 1965), p. 70.

[2] Wittgenstein, L., Letter to Malcolm, December, 1945, quoted in Malcolm, N., *Ludwig Wittgenstein: A Memoir* (London: Oxford University Press, 1958), p. 45.

Part Two: In Freud's Defense

[1] *Moses and Monotheism: Three Essays.* (1939). In *The Origins of Religion,* Harmondsworth: Penguin Books Ltd., 1985, pp. 349-350.

[2] "The Direction of the Treatment and the Principles of Its Power." In *Ecrits: A Selection,* London: Tavistock Publications Ltd., 1977, p. 235.

[3] Freud, S. "Obsessive Actions and Religious Practices" (1907). In *The Origins of Religion,* Harmondsworth: Penguin Books Ltd., 1985, p. 37.

[4] "The expenditure of force on the part of the physician was evidently the measure of a *resistance* on the part of the patient. It was only necessary to translate into words what I myself had observed, and I was in possession of the theory of *repression.*

It was now easy to reconstruct the pathogenic process." Freud, S. *An Autobiographical Study*. (1925). New York: W. W. Norton and Co., 1963, p.49.

5 Freud, S. *Totem and Taboo*. (1913). In *The Origins of Religion*, p. 50.

6 Freud, S. *The Future of An Illusion*. (1927). New York: W. W. Norton and Co., 1961, p. 56.

7 *Inhibitions, Symptoms and Anxiety*. (1926). Harmondsworth: Penguin Books Ltd., 1979, p. 296.

8 *Ibid.*, pp. 300-301.

9 Freud, S. "My Contact with Josef Popper-Lynkeus" (1932). In *Character and Culture*, New York: Macmillan Publishing Co., 1963, p. 303.

10 Freud, S. "Delusions and Dreams in Jensen's *Gradiva*" (1907). *Standard Edition, IX*, p.85.

11 Freud, S. "Some Psychical Consequences of the Anatomical Distinction Between the Sexes" (1925). In *On Sexuality*, Harmondsworth: Penguin Books Ltd., 1977, pp. 323-343.

12 *The Future of an Illusion*, p. 11.

13 Freud, S. *The Ego and the Id*. (1923). New York: W. W. Norton and Co., 1962, pp. 23-24.

14 "The Psychogenesis of a Case of Homosexuality in a Woman" (1920). In *Case Histories II*, Harmondsworth: Penguin Books Ltd., 1979, p. 395.

15 "The Taboo of Virginity" (1918). In *On Sexuality*, p. 270.

16 *Inhibitions, Symptoms and Anxiety*, p. 286.

17 *Ibid.*, p. 326.

18 *Ibid.*, p. 295.

19 "A special function was instituted which had periodically to search the outer world, in order that its data might be already familiar if an urgent inner need should arise; this function was *attention*. Its activity meets the sense-impressions halfway, instead of awaiting their appearance. At the same time there was probably introduced a system of *notation*, whose task was to deposit the results of this periodical activity of consciousness — a part of that which we call *memory*." Freud, S. "Formulations regarding the Two Principles in Mental Functioning" (1911). In *General Psychological Theory*, New York: Macmillan Publishing Co., 1963, p. 23.

20 *Inhibitions, Symptoms and Anxiety*, p. 327.

21 "Two Principles in Mental Functioning," p. 24.

22 Freud, S. *Civilization and its Discontents*. (1930). New York: W. W. Norton and Co., 1961, p. 14.

23 "In anxiety-hysteria a preliminary phase of the process is frequently overlooked, perhaps indeed is really omitted; on careful observation, however, it can be clearly discerned. It consists in anxiety appearing without the subject knowing what he is afraid of.... Then at some repetition of this process a first step was taken in the direction of

mastering this distressing development of anxiety. The fugitive cathexis attached itself to a substitutive idea which, on the one hand, was connected by association with the rejected idea, and, on the other, escaped repression by reason of its remoteness from that idea (displacement-substitute), and which permitted of a rationalization of the still uncontrollable outbreak of anxiety. The substitutive idea now plays the part of an anti-cathexis for the system Cs (Pcs) by securing that system against an emergence into consciousness of the repressed idea; on the other hand, it is, or acts as if it were, the point at which the anxiety-affect, which is now all the more uncontrollable, may break out and be discharged.... The substitutive idea acts in the one instance as a conductor from the system Ucs to the system Cs; in the other instance, as an independent source for the release of anxiety." "The Unconscious" (1915), in *General Psychological Theory*, pp. 130-131.

[24] "A negative judgement is the intellectual substitute for repression; the 'No' in which it is expressed is the hallmark of repression, a certificate of origin, as it were, like 'Made in Germany'. By the help of the symbol of negation, the thinking-process frees itself from the limitations of repression and enriches itself with the subject-matter without which it could not work efficiently. ...Expressed in the language of the oldest, that is, of the oral, instinctual impulses, the alternative runs thus: 'I should like to eat that, or I should like to spit it out'; or, carried a stage further: 'I should like to take this into me and keep that out of me.' That is to say, it is to be either *inside* me or *outside* me." "Negation" (1925), in *General Psychological Theory*, pp. 214-215.

[25] Freud. S. *The Question of Lay Analysis*. (1926). *Standard Edition*, XX, p. 187.

[26] *The Ego and the Id*, p. 49.

[27] "...let us state definitely that it is not even correct to suppose that repression withholds from consciousness all the derivatives of what was primally repressed. If these derivatives are sufficiently far removed from the repressed instinct-presentation, whether owing to the process of distortion or by reason of the number of intermediate associations, they have free access to consciousness. It is as though the resistance of consciousness against them was in inverse proportion to their remoteness from what was originally repressed... Indeed, the associations which we require him (the patient) to give, while refraining from any consciously directed train of thought or any criticism, and from which we reconstruct a conscious interpretation of the repressed instinct-presentation, are precisely derivatives of this kind...

...Repression acts...in a *highly specific* manner in each instance; every single derivative of the repressed may have its peculiar fate — a little more or a little less distortion alters the whole issue. In this connection it becomes comprehensible that those objects to which men give their pref-

erence, that is, their ideals, originate in the same perceptions and experiences as those objects of which they have most abhorrence, and that the
two originally differed from one another only by slight modifications. Indeed, as we found in the origin of the fetish, it is possible for the original
instinct-presentation to be split into two, one part undergoing repression, while the remainder, just on account of its intimate association with
the other, undergoes idealization." "Repression" (1915), in *General Psychological Theory*, pp. 107-108, my parenthesis.

28 *The Future of an Illusion*, p. 55.

29 "When does the Oedipus complex, according to Freud, go into its
Untergang, that decisive event for all of the subject's subsequent development? When the subject feels the threat of castration, and feels it from
both directions implied by the Oedipal triangle. If he wants to take his
mother's place, the same thing will happen — remember that he is aware
of the fact that the woman is castrated, this perception marking the
completion and maturity of the Oedipus complex. Thus, with regard to
the phallus, the subject is caught in an impossible dilemma with no
avenue of escape." Lacan, J. "Desire and the Interpretation of Desire in
Hamlet". In Shoshana Felman (Ed.), *Literature and Psychoanalysis: The
Question of Reading: Otherwise*. Baltimore: The Johns Hopkins University
Press, 1982, p. 46. This may be compared with Nietzsche's statements
that rationality is founded upon error and that rationality is a trap from
which there is no escape.

30 *The Question of Lay Analysis*, p. 194.

31 "Some Psychical Consequences of the Anatomical Distinction Between
the Sexes".

32 "...we think of the pain which defloration causes a virgin, and we are
perhaps even inclined to consider this factor as decisive and to give up
the search for any others. But we cannot well ascribe such importance to
this pain, we must rather substitute for it the narcissistic injury which
proceeds from the destruction of an organ and which is even represented
in a rationalized form in the knowledge that loss of virginity brings a
diminution of sexual value. The marriage customs of primitive peoples,
however, contain a warning against over-estimating this. We have heard
that in some cases the rite falls into two phases... and this proves to us
that the purpose of the taboo observance is not fulfilled by avoiding anatomical defloration, that the husband is to be spared something else as
well as the woman's reaction to the painful injury." "The Taboo of
Virginity" (1918), in *On Sexuality*, pp. 275-276.

33 "Thus the phallus is this thing that is presented by Freud as the key to the
Untergang of the Oedipus complex. I say 'thing' and not 'object', because
it is a real thing, one that has not yet been made a symbol, but that has the
potential of becoming one.

"Freud's presentation of the problem puts the female child in a situation that is not at all dissymetrical with that of the male. With respect to this thing, the subject enters into a relationship that we may call one of lassitude — the word is in Freud's text — where gratification is concerned. As for the boy, he decides he's just not up to it. And as for the girl, she gives up any expectation of gratification in this way — the renunciation is expressed even more clearly in her case than in his. All we can say is expressed in a formulation that doesn't come out in Freud's text but whose pertinence is everywhere indicated: the Oedipus complex goes into its decline insofar as the subject must mourn the phallus." Lacan, J., ibid.

34 "When now I announce that the fetish is a substitute for the penis, I shall certainly create disappointment; so I hasten to add that it is not a substitute for any chance penis, but for a particular and quite special penis that had been extremely important in early childhood but had later been lost. That is to say, it should normally have been given up, but the fetish is precisely designed to preserve it from extinction. To put it more plainly, the fetish is a substitute for the woman's (the mother's) penis that the little boy once believed in and — for reasons familiar to us — does not want to give up." "Fetishism" (1927), in On Sexuality, pp. 351-352.

35 The Future of an Illusion, p. 53.

36 "Obsessive Actions and Religious Practices," pp. 38-39.

37 "Psychoanalysis and the War Neuroses," (1919), in Character and Culture, p. 219.

38 "The Relation of the Poet to Day-Dreaming," (1908), in Character and Culture, p. 36.

39 Freud, S. The Interpretation of Dreams. Harmondsworth: Penguin Books Ltd., 1976, p. 771.

40 "Negation," p. 217.

41 "Clearly the repression of the Oedipus complex was no easy task. The child's parents, and especially his father, were perceived as the obstacle to a realization of his Oedipus wishes; so his infantile ego fortified itself for the carrying out of the repression by erecting this same obstacle within itself. It borrowed strength to do this, so to speak, from the father, and this loan was an extraordinarily momentous act. The super-ego retains the character of the father... I shall presently... bring forward a suggestion about the source of its power to dominate in this way — the source, that is, of its compulsive character which manifests itself in the form of a categorical imperative." The Ego and the Id, pp. 24-25. The suggestion about the source of conscience and guilt is that the death drive manifests itself in the aggressivity of the super-ego.

Furthermore, "If it is really the super-ego which, in humour, speaks such kindly words of comfort to the intimidated ego, this teaches us that we have still very much to learn about the nature of that energy... Finally, if the super-ego does try to comfort the ego by humour and to protect it from suffering, this does not conflict with its derivation from the parental function." "Humour" (1928), in *Character and Culture*, pp. 268-269.

[42] "Reflections upon War and Death" (1915), in *Character and Culture*, p. 115.

[43] "Shortly before I wrote this study it seemed as though my life would soon be brought to an end by the recurrence of a malignant disease; but surgical skill saved me in 1923 and I was able to continue my life and my work, though no longer in freedom from pain. In the period of more than ten years that has passed since then, I have never ceased my analytic work nor my writing... But I myself find that a significant change has come about. Threads which in the course of my development had become intertangled have now begun to separate; interests which I had acquired in the later part of my life have receded, while the older and original ones become prominent once more. It is true that in this last decade I have carried out some important pieces of analytic work, such as the revision of the problem of anxiety in my book *Hemmung, Symptom und Angst* (published in 1926) or the simple explanation of sexual 'fetishism' which I was able to make in 1927. Nevertheless it would be true to say that, since I put forward my hypothesis of the existence of two kinds of instinct (Eros and the death instinct) and since I proposed a division of the mental personality into an ego, a super-ego, and an id (in 1923), I have made no further decisive contributions to psychoanalysis: what I have written on the subject since then has been either unessential or would soon have been supplied by someone else. This circumstance is connected with an alteration in myself, with what might have been described as a phase of regressive development. My interest, after making a lifelong *detour* through the natural sciences, medicine and psychotherapy, returned to the cultural problems which had fascinated me long before, when I was a youth scarcely old enough for thinking....I perceived ever more clearly that the events of human history, the interactions between human nature, cultural development and the precipitates of primaeval experiences (the most prominent example of which is religion) are no more than a reflection of the dynamic conflicts between the ego, the id, and the super-ego, which psychoanalysis studies in the individual —are the very same processes repeated upon a wider stage. In *The Future of an Illusion* I expressed an essentially negative valuation of religion. Later, I found a formula which did better justice to it: while granting that its power lies in the truth which it contains, I showed that that truth was not a material but a historical truth." Postscript (1935) to *An Autobiographical Study*, pp. 122-124.

[44] "Dostoevsky and Parricide" (1928), in *Character and Culture*, pp. 283-284.

[45] "We are aware that the demand for renunciation of instinct, and its en-

forcement, call forth hostility and aggressive impulses, which only in a later phase of psychical development become transformed into a sense of guilt." "The Acquisition of Power over Fire" (1932), in *Character and Culture*, p. 297.

And, "We shall not be wrong, perhaps, in saying that the weak point in the ego's organisation seems to lie in its attitude to the sexual function, as though the biological antithesis between self-preservation and the preservation of the species had found a psychological expression at this point." Freud, S. *An Outline of Psychoanalysis* (1940), *Standard Edition*, XXIII, p. 186.

[46] *Totem and Taboo*, p. 122.

[47] Sophocles, *The Theban Plays*, Trans. E.F. Watling, (Harmondsworth: Penguin Books Ltd., 1947), pp. 62 and 68.

[48] Wittgenstein, Ludwig, *Tractatus Logico-Philosophicus* (London: Routledge & Kegan Paul, 1961), Sec. 6.43, p. 72.

[49] *The Future of an Illusion*, p. 36.

[50] "He had succeeded in subjecting his feelings to the yoke of research and in inhibiting their free utterance; but even for him there were occasions when what had been suppressed obtained expression forcibly. The death of the mother he had once loved so dearly was one of these. What we have before us in the account of the costs of the funeral is the expression — distorted out of all recognition — of his mourning for his mother.... But similar processes are well known to us in the abnormal conditions of neurosis and especially of what is known as 'obsessional neurosis'.... The expression of these repressed feelings has been lowered by the forces opposed to them to such a degree that one would have had to form a most insignificant estimate of their intensity; but the imperative compulsiveness with which this trivial expressive act is performed betrays the real force of the impulses — a force which is rooted in the unconscious and which consciousness would like to deny. Only a comparison such as this with what happens in obsessional neurosis can explain Leonardo's account of the expenses of his mother's funeral. In his unconscious he was still tied to her by erotically coloured feelings, as he had been in childhood." Freud, S. *Leonardo da Vinci and a Memory of His Childhood* (1910). New York: W.W. Norton and Co., 1964, p. 55.

And, "Of the three conditioning factors in melancholia —loss of the object, ambivalence, and repression of libido into the ego— the first two are found also in the obsessional reproaches arising after the death of loved persons. In these it is indubitably the ambivalence that motivates the conflict, and observation shows that after it has run its course nothing in the nature of a triumph or a manic state of mind is left." "Mourning and Melancholia" (1917), in *General Psychological Theory*, p. 179.

And, "Now, I think, we can at last grasp two things perfectly clearly: the part played by love in the origin of conscience and the fatal inevitability of the sense of guilt. Whether one has killed one's father or has abstained from doing so is not really the decisive thing. One is bound to feel guilty in either case, for the sense of gullt is an expression of the conflict due to ambivalence, of the eternal struggle between Eros and the instinct of destruction or death. This conflict is set going as soon as men are faced with the task of living together." *Civilization and Its Discontents*, p. 89.

This may be compared with notes 41 and 43, as confirming Freud's account of the development of the changes in his outlook between 1923 and 1935.This in turn lends significance to his comment on Goethe which closely follows the last quotation from *Civilization and Its Discontents* above: "And we may well heave a sigh of relief at the thought that it is nevertheless vouchsafed to a few to salvage without effort from the whirlpool of their own feelings the deepest truths, towards which the rest of us have to find our way through tormenting uncertainty and with restless groping"(p. 90).

[51] Freud, S. *Group Psychology and the Analysis of the Ego.* (1921). New York: W. W. Norton and Co., 1959.

[52] *Ibid.*, p. 55.

[53] "Thought... is essentially an experimental way of acting, accompanied by displacement of smaller quantities of cathexis together with less expenditure (discharge) of them. For this purpose conversion of free cathexis into 'bound' cathexes was imperative, and this was brought about by means of raising the level of the whole cathectic process. It is probable that thinking was originally unconscious, in so far as it rose above mere ideation and turned to the relations between the object-impressions, and that it became endowed with further qualities which were perceptible to consciousness only through its connection with the memory-traces of words." "Two Principles in Mental Functioning," p. 24.

[54] *Totem and Taboo*, pp. 221-222.

[55] "The Theme of the Three Caskets" (1913), in *Character and Culture*, p. 69.

[56] *Ibid.*, pp. 74-75.

[57] *Ibid.*, p. 76.

[58] "The Resistances to Psychoanalysis" (1925), in *Character and Culture*, p. 261.

[59] *Civilization and Its Discontents*, p. 78.

[60] "In psychoanalysis there is no choice for us but to declare mental processes to be in themselves unconscious, and to compare the perception of them by consciousness with the perception of the outside world through the sense-organs; we even hope to extract some fresh knowledge from the comparison. The psychoanalytic assumption of unconscious mental activity appears to us, on the one hand, a further development of that primitive animism which caused our own consciousness to be reflected

in all around us, and, on the other hand, it seems to be an extension of the corrections begun by Kant in regard to our views on external perception. Just as Kant warned us not to overlook the fact that our perception is subjectively conditioned and must not be regarded as identical with the phenomena perceived but never really discerned, so psychoanalysis bids us not to set conscious perception in the place of the unconscious mental process which is its object. The mental, like the physical, is not necessarily in reality just what it appears to us to be." "The Unconscious," p. 121. The path of the involution or invagination can be traced in this passage alone, either with respect to the history of thought, or to the logic displayed by Freud's conception of the movement of this history — a kind of zig-zag — or with respect to the interplay of both of these, which finds its nodal point — its navel — at the spot where the psychoanalyst introduces mention of the contribution of psychoanalysis, that is, at the beginning and at the end.

[61] "...All that is language is lent from this otherness and this is why the subject is always a fading thing that runs under the chain of signifiers. For the definition of a signifier is that it represents a subject not for another subject but for another signifier. This is the only definition possible of the signifier as different from the sign. The sign is something that represents something for somebody, but the signifier is something that represents a subject for another signifier. The consequence is that the subject disappears exactly as in the case of the two unitary traits, while under the second signifier appears what is called meaning or signification; and then in sequence the other signifiers appear and other significations.

"The question of desire is that the fading subject yearns to find itself again by means of some sort of encounter with this miraculous thing defined by the phantasm. In its endeavor it is sustained by that which I call the lost object that I evoked in the beginning — which is such a terrible thing for the imagination. That which is produced and maintained here, and which in my vocabulary I call the object, lower case, *a*, is well known by all psychoanalysts as all psychoanalysis is founded on the existence of this peculiar object. But the relation between this barred subject with this object (*a*) is the structure which is always found in the phantasm which supports desire, in as much as desire is only that which I have called the metonymy of all signification.

"In this brief presentation I have tried to show you what the question of the structure is inside the psychoanalytical reality. I have not, however, said anything about such dimensions as the imaginary and the symbolical. It is, of course, absolutely essential to understand how the symbolic order can enter inside the *veçu*, lived experience, of mental life, but I cannot tonight put forth such an explanation. Consider, however, that which is at the same time the least known and the most certain fact about this mythical subject which is the sensible phase of the living being: this fathomless thing capable of experiencing something between birth and death, capable of covering the whole spectrum of pain and pleasure in a word, what in French we call the *sujet de la jouissance*. When I came here this evening I saw on the little neon sign the motto 'Enjoy Coca-Cola.' It reminded me that in English, I think, there is no term to designate precisely this enormous weight of meaning which is in the French word *jouissance* — or in the Latin *fruor*. In the dictionary I looked up *jouir* and found 'to possess, to use,' but it is not that at all. If the living being is something at all thinkable, it will be above all as subject of the *jouissance*; but this psychological law that we call the pleasure principle (and which is only the principle of displeasure) is very soon to create a barrier to all *jouissance*. If I am enjoying myself a little too much, I begin to feel pain and I moderate my pleasures. The organism seems made to avoid too much *jouissance*. Probably we would all be as quiet as oysters if it were not for this curious organization which forces us to disrupt the barrier of pleasure or perhaps only makes us dream of forcing and disrupting this barrier. All that is elaborated by the subjective construction on the scale of the signifier in its relation to the Other and which has its root in language is only there to permit the full spectrum of desire to allow us to approach, to test, this sort of forbidden *jouissance* which is the only valuable meaning that is offered to our life." Lacan, J. "Of Structure as an Inmixing of an Otherness Prerequisite to Any Subject Whatever." In Macksey, R. and Donato, E. (Eds.), *The Structuralist Controversy, The Languages of Criticism and the Sciences of Man*, Baltimore: The Johns Hopkins University Press, 1972, pp. 194-195. This passage is relevant too to the passage quoted from Freud in the light of the accompanying comment, in the preceding footnote.

[62] *Analysis of a Phobia in a Five-Year-Old Boy*. (1909). In Freud, S., *Case Histories I*, Harmondsworth: Penguin Books Ltd., 1977, p. 301.

[63] " 'My eagle is awake and, like me, does honour to the sun. With eagle's claws it reaches out for the new light. You are my rightful animals: I love you.

" 'But I still lack my rightful men!' " Nietzsche, F. *Thus Spoke Zarathustra*. Harmondsworth: Penguin Books Ltd., 1961, 1969, p. 334.

And, "Oh life's midday! Oh second youth! Oh garden of summer! I wait in restless ecstasy, I stand and watch and wait — it is friends I await, in readiness day and night, *new* friends. Come now! It is time you were here!

"*This* song is done — desire's sweet cry died on the lips: a sorcerer did it, the timely friend, the midday friend — no! ask not who he is — at midday it happened, at midday one became two...

"Now, sure of victory together, we celebrate the feast of feasts: friend *Zarathustra* has come, the guest of guests! Now the world is laughing, the

dread curtain is rent, the wedding day has come for light and dark-
ness..." Nietzsche, F. *Beyond Good and Evil*. Harmondsworth: Penguin
Books Ltd., 1973, p. 204.

[64] *Civilization and Its Discontents*, p. 53, translator's parenthesis.

[65] "Bisexuality! I am sure you are right about it. And I am accustoming
myself to regarding every sexual act as an event between four individuals." Freud, Letter 113 to Fliess, in the editor's note to p. 23 of *The Ego and
the Id.*

And, "At the dissolution of the Oedipus complex the four trends of
which it consists will group themselves in such a way as to produce a father-identification and a mother-identification. The father-identification
will preserve the object-relation to the mother which belonged to the
positive complex, and will at the same time replace the object-relation to
the father which belonged to the inverted complex, and the same will be
true, *mutatis mutandis*, of the mother-identification. The relative intensity
of the two identifications in any individual will reflect the preponder-
ance in him of one or other of the two sexual dispositions.

*"The broad general outcome of the sexual phase dominated by the Oedipus
complex may, therefore, be taken to be the forming of a precipitate in the ego,
consisting of these two identifications in some way united with each other. This
modification of the ego retains its special position; it confronts the other contents
of the ego as an ego ideal or super-ego.*

"The super-ego is, however, not simply a residue of of the earliest object
choices of the id; it also represents an energetic reaction-formation
against those choices." *The Ego and the Id*, p. 24.

[66] On the sexual instincts: "At their first appearance they support themselves
upon the instincts of self-preservation, from which they only gradually
detach themselves; in their choice of object also they follow paths indicated by the ego-instincts. Some of them remain throughout life associated with these latter and furnish them with libidinal components...
They have this distinctive characteristic — that they have in a high degree
the capacity to act vicariously for one another and that they can readily
change their objects. In consequence of the last-mentioned properties
they are capable of activities widely removed from their original modes
of attaining their aims (sublimation).

"...Observation shows us that an instinct may undergo the following
vicissitudes:

    Reversal into its opposite,
    Turning round upon the subject,
    Repression,
    Sublimation."

"Instincts and Their Vicissitudes" (1915), in *General Psychological Theory*, pp. 90-91.

[67] *Totem and Taboo*, pp. 122-123.
[68] *Group Psychology and the Analysis of the Ego*, p. 53.
[69] *The Ego and the Id*, p. 27.
[70] *Civilization and Its Discontents*, p. 61.
[71] *Ibid.*, pp. 67-68. "It would be easy to suppose, then, that as a result of the
ceaseless impact of external stimuli on the surface of the vesicle, its
substance to a certain depth may have become permanently modified...
In terms of the system *Cs.*, this would mean that its elements could
undergo no further permanent modification from the passage of excitation...: now, however, they would have become capable of giving rise to
consciousness... It may be supposed that... diminution of resistance... is
what lays down a permanent trace of the excitation... In the system *Cs.*,
then, resistance of this kind to passage from one element to another
would no longer exist.... the elements of the system *Cs.* would carry no
bound energy but only energy capable of free discharge. It seems best,
however, to express oneself as cautiously as possible on these points....
"...This little fragment of living substance is suspended in the middle
of an external world charged with the most powerful energies; and it
would be killed by the stimulation emanating from these if it were not
provided with a protective shield against stimuli...: its outermost surface
ceases to have the structure proper to living matter, becomes to some degree inorganic... By its death, the outer layer has saved all the deeper
ones from a similar fate... *Protection against* stimuli is an almost more important function for the living organism than *reception of* stimuli...
"...our abstract idea of time seems to be wholly derived from the
method of working of the system *Pcpt.–Cs.*.... This mode of functioning
may perhaps constitute another way of providing a shield against stimuli. I know that these remarks must sound very obscure, but I must limit
myself to these hints.
"...The higher the system's own quiescent cathexis, the greater seems
to be its binding force; conversely, the lower its cathexis, the less capacity will it have for taking up inflowing energy... we have to distinguish
between... a freely flowing cathexis that presses on towards discharge
and a quiescent cathexis. We may perhaps suspect that the binding of the
energy that streams into the mental apparatus consists in its change from
a freely flowing into a quiescent state.
"...Again, it is easy to identify the primary psychical process with
Breuer's freely mobile cathexis and the secondary process with changes
in his bound or tonic cathexis. If so, it would be the task of the higher
strata of the mental apparatus to bind the instinctual excitation reaching
the primary process. A failure to effect this binding would provoke a dis-
turbance analogous to a traumatic neurosis; and only after the binding
has been accomplished would it be possible for the dominance of the

pleasure principle (and of its modification, the reality principle) to proceed unhindered. Till then the other task of the mental apparatus, the task of mastering or binding excitations, would have precedence — not, indeed, in *opposition* to the pleasure principle, but independently of it and to some extent in disregard of it." Freud, S. *Beyond the Pleasure Principle.* (1920). New York: W. W. Norton and Co., 1961, pp. 20-29. Consciousness seems to be situated, decisively and exclusively in each case, on both sides of the bound/free distinction. Or, if we keep consciousness constant, then the bound and free states periodically appear each in the other's place, as is also the case with living and dead substance. Between the impossibly organised play, in its self-undercutting sequence of arrival and departure, of both of these sets of switches, is perhaps to be found the movement of Freud's resistance, resistance perhaps being nothing but a movement, which slides inexorably between the terms it produces.

[72] "The Moses of Michelangelo" (1914), in *Character and Culture*, p. 92.

[73] *Totem and Taboo*, pp. 83-84. This may be suggestively compared with note 43.

[74] *Ibid.*, p. 83 note 2.

[75] *Beyond the Pleasure Principle*, p. 51.

[76] "This aggressive instinct is the derivative and the main representative of the death instinct which we have found alongside of Eros and which shares world-dominion with it. And now, I think, the meaning of the evolution of civilization is no longer obscure to us. It must present the struggle between Eros and Death, between the instinct of life and the instinct of destruction, as it works itself out in the human species. This struggle is what all life essentially consists of, and the evolution of civilization may therefore be simply described as the struggle for life of the human species. And it is this battle of the giants that our nurse-maids try to appease with their lullaby about Heaven." *Civilization and Its Discontents*, p. 77. Freud adds in a footnote to this passage, "And we may probably add more precisely, a struggle for life in the shape it was bound to assume after a certain event which still remains to be discovered." (*Ibid.*).

[77] "Most of them are organized in such a way as to fall into two divisions, known as marriage-classes or 'phratries'. Each of these phratries is exogamous and comprises a number of totem clans. As a rule each phratry is further subdivided into two 'sub-phratries', the whole tribe being thus divided into four, with the sub-phratries intermediate between the phratries and the totem clans." *Totem and Taboo*, p. 60.

[78] See, for an appreciation of broken rings and time, Yeats, W. B., "The Wild Swans at Coole" In *Collected Poems of W. B. Yeats*, London: Macmillan London Ltd., 1950, pp. 147-148. This poem published in 1919.

[79] *Totem and Taboo*, p. 89.

[80] "Dismembered limbs, a severed head, a hand cut off at the wrist, ... feet which dance by themselves... — all these have something peculiarly uncanny about them, especially when, as in the last instance, they prove capable of independent activity in addition. As we already know, this kind of uncanniness springs from its proximity to the castration complex. To some people the idea of being buried alive by mistake is the most uncanny thing of all. And yet psycho-analysis has taught us that this terrifying phantasy is only a transformation of another phantasy which had originally nothing terrifying about it at all, but was qualified by a certain lasciviousness — the phantasy, I mean, of intra-uterine existence." Freud, S. "The Uncanny" (1919), *Standard Edition, XVII*, p. 244.

It should perhaps be noted that Heidegger did *assert* a sharp distinction between the two knowledges or, perhaps, experiences in *Being and Time₁*, where the assertion that the inauthentic is prior to the authentic is particularly noteworthy. This work, read in the light of his later work, presumably displays the same kind of modernity relative to that later work as Freud's *Project* does in the light of Freud's later work.

[81] *Totem and Taboo*, p. 214.

[82] *Beyond the Pleasure Principle*, pp. 53-54.

[83] "It is only a small detail, and anyone who was not a psycho-analyst would attach no importance to it. He might not even notice it, and if his attention was drawn to it he might say that a thing like that can happen to anyone in a moment of distraction or of strong feeling, and that it has no further significance.

"The psycho-analyst thinks differently. To him nothing is too small to be a manifestation of hidden mental processes. He has learnt long ago that such case of forgetting or repetition are significant, and that it is the 'distraction' which allows impulses that are otherwise hidden to be revealed." *Leonardo da Vinci and a Memory of His Childhood*, p. 69. Freud supports his statement with the following quote from Dante's *Paradiso*:

" 'He who usurps on earth my place, my place, my place, which in the presence of the Son of God is vacant, has made a sewer of the ground where I am buried.' " (*ibid.*, p. 70).

[84] *Totem and Taboo*, p. 151, my transliteration of Ananke from the Greek, translator's parenthesis.

[85] *The Future of An Illusion* pp. 23-24, translator's parentheses.

[86] "A Religious Experience," (1928), in *Character and Culture*, pp. 272-273.

[87] "The Resistances to Psychoanalysis," pp. 258-259.

Introduction to Part Three

[1] Richards, I.A., *The Philosophy of Rhetoric*. New York: Oxford University Press, 1964, p. 86.

[2] Wilde, O., *Complete Works of Oscar Wilde*. (Vyvyan Holland, Ed.) London: Collins, 1966. "Phrases and Philosophies for the Use of the Young," p. 1206.

[3] Wilde, O., "A Few Maxims for the Instruction of the Over-Educated," in *Complete Works*, p. 1203.

Part Three: The Impotence of Being Earnest

[1] Plato, *Phaedrus*, 256a-257b. In Hamilton, E., and Cairns, H. (eds.), *Plato: The Collected Dialogues*. Princeton: Princeton University Press, 1961, pp. 501–502.

COLUMBUS & OTHER CANNIBALS
THE WÉTIKO DISEASE & THE WHITE MAN
JACK D. FORBES

A noted American Indian scholar and activist
examines the heritage of indigenous American
cultures since the coming of Europeans in the
15th century, with a particular focus on the
"wétiko disease," the White Man's fascination
with the exploitation and control of nature
and his fellow man.
Spring, 1991 — $12 postpaid

"GONE TO CROATAN"
ORIGINS OF AMERICAN DROPOUT CULTURE
JAMES KOEHNLINE & PETER LAMBORN WILSON, EDITORS

Studies of lost American history and the cultures
of disappearance, including "tri-racial isolate"
communities, the bucaneers, "white Indians,"
black Islamic movements, the Maroons of the
Great Dismal Swamp, scandalous eugenics
theories, rural "hippie" communes, and many other
aspects of American autonomous cultures.
A *festschrift* in honor of historian Hugo Leaming
Bey of the Moorish Science Temple.
Spring, 1991 — $12 postpaid